Canada

Decentralized

Can our nation survive?

**Examining the dire implications
of stripping away federal powers**

I0094148

Michael B. Davie

Manor House Publishing Inc.

For
Philippa

Canadian Cataloguing in Publication Data:

Davie, Michael B.

Canada Decentralized:
Can our Nation Survive?

Examining the dire implications
of stripping away federal powers

Includes bibliographical references and index

ISBN 0-9685803-3-5

1. Decentralization in government - Canada. 2. Federal-provincial relations - Canada. I. Title.

JL19.D39 2000   320.471   C00-901621-X

Published October 2000
by Manor House Publishing Inc.
(905) 648-2193.

Printed in Canada by Friesens Corporation

Great books by Michael B. Davie

Canada Decentralized MH
Can our Nation Survive?

Quebec and Section 33 MH
Why the Notwithstanding Clause must Not Stand

Inside the Witches' Coven MH
Exploring Wiccan Rituals

Enterprise 2000 MH
Hamilton, Halton and Niagara Embrace the New
Millennium

Success Stories BR
Business Achievement in Greater Hamilton and
Beyond

Hamilton: It's Happening* BR
Celebrating Hamilton's Sesquicentennial

MH = Published by Manor House Publishing.
BR = Published by BRaSH Publishing
* = With co-author Sherry Sleightholm

Manor House Publishing
(905)-648-2193

About the Author

Michael B. Davie is a veteran political observer who previously wrote Quebec And Section 33: Why The Notwithstanding Clause Should Not Stand.

The award-winning writer previously wrote *Enterprise 2000* and *Success Stories*. He also wrote over 100 business profiles and some chapter text as co-author of *Hamilton: It's Happening,* commemorating Hamilton's 150th anniversary.

Michael B. Davie is also a writer/editor with The Toronto Star, Canada's largest-circulation newspaper reaching millions of Canadian readers daily.

He has won literally dozens of awards for outstanding journalism and is a prolific freelance writer whose work reaches an international audience.

In addition to publications in the United States and Europe, his work has appeared with and without bylines in many major Canadian publications, including the Halifax Chronicle-Herald, Montreal Gazette, Winnipeg Free Press, Edmonton Journal, Calgary Herald and Vancouver Sun.

Prior to joining The Star, he was an editor with The Globe and Mail, Canada's national newspaper with coast-to-coast-to-coast readership.

Previous to The Globe, he spent 17 years as a reporter editor and columnist with The Hamilton Spectator, a big regional daily, which published thousands of his articles.

He won 27 national, provincial and regional awards and citations of merit for outstanding journalism.

While with The Spectator, Michael B. Davie spent a decade writing for the newspaper's Business section where he wrote hundreds of inspiring business profiles. Hundreds of his articles have also appeared in American Metal Market, Iron & Steelmaker, North American Steel Journal and Marketing magazines.

Prior to joining The Spectator, the author spent five years working for other publications, including The Welland Tribune, a mid-sized daily where he provided business and political coverage as a reporter, columnist and editor.

Before The Tribune, he had served two years as regional news editor for one of Ontario's largest chains of community newspapers.

His interest in writing began in childhood and as a teenage in the late 1960s to early 1970s his work began appearing in small, high school and counter-culture publications.

He turned professional in the mid-1970s as Editor of The Phoenix serving Mohawk College of Applied Arts & Technology where he earned a Broadcast Journalism diploma.

He also holds a Niagara College Print Journalism diploma and degrees in Political Science from McMaster University where he was repeatedly named to the Deans' Honour List and won the Political Science Prize for outstanding academic achievement.

Among the many journalism awards he's earned are several Western Ontario Newspapers Association awards for exemplary business writing. He earned his most recent WONA Business Writing award in 1997. The same year, he received, in n Vancouver, a national Lifetime Achievement Award for journalism.

Born and raised in Hamilton, he currently resides in Ancaster with his wife Philippa and their children Donovan, Sarah and Ryan.

Belated Credit for Past Work:

Please note: Regarding the book Enterprise 2000: Greater Hamilton, Halton and Niagara embrace the New Millennium, author Michael B. Davie should have received credit for the concept and design of the book's striking cover depicting a limitless horizon with, in the foreground, a New Year's baby seated at a computer with the image repeated endlessly on the computer screen.

He also originated the back cover concept of the author leaning on the computer monitor showing the baby image, again repeated endlessly.

Photographer Paul Sparrow should have received credit for bringing these images to realization through his skillful photographic and computer montage work. These works by both gentlemen are hereby recognized.

– Manor House Publishing Inc.

CONTENTS

Acknowledgements

This book would not have been possible without the works of many distinguished political scientists whose words of wisdom lend my own work a good deal of substance and corroberation. I highly recommend reading any of the books cited in the bibliography to gain a fuller understanding of Canadian politics and the Quebec Problem. My thanks, as always, to my wife Philippa and our children for their words of encouragment and support concerning my various writing endeavours. - Michael B. Davie.

INTRODUCTION

The hidden threat
of decentralization:

Can Canada survive
a steady loss of power?

Decentralization. The word alone is enough to
make one's eyes gloss over – but that would be a
mistake. A very costly mistake.

Canadians – via successive federal governments –
have been sleepwalking into a looming catastrophy of
decentralization.

Outnumbered 10 to one by provincial governments, federal government after federal government
has tried to make peace with the provinces, often by
ceding various federal powers to them. That, in a
nutshell, is how decentralization happens: The central
(federal) government decentralizes power by giving
powers to the provinces.

How is decentralization a threat to Canada? To put it quite blunty: Why should we care?

At a glance, decentralization doesn't appear to be a threat at all. It may even give the appearance of being a good thing. After all, many Canadians in our huge country feel isolated from Ottawa.

These Canadians are physically, perhaps even emotionally, closer to their provincial government. This is true even for many people in Ontario and Quebec. It is more likely to be true for people living in other provincies who have far more geography between themselves and Ottawa.

Beyond the separation of land mass, there is a widely held belief provincial governments are closer in structure to being local governments and are more responsive to the needs of people in their given province.

Such feelings of closeness to one's province may be valid. Provincial governments may, in many matters, be more responsive than the federal government could ever hope to be.
Yet these assumptions – even if they're correct – are largely irrelvant when determining the threat of decentralization. They're irrelevant, because, when it comes to addressing many aspects of our day-to-day l. Health care is a major concern for many Canadians. It's under the jurisdiction of the provinces. Education is also a provincial matter.

Even such mundane matters as local roads and sewers handled by municipal governments and school boards are provincial in nature: The municipalities and boards are creations of the provinces and are controlled by provincial governments. In short, the provinces can be as responsive as they want in matters within their own jursidiction and control.

However, many of these same Canadians - who remain convinced their provincial government is closer to them – also value a strong federal government.

Canadians want and expect their federal government to represent Canada and Canadian interests on the world stage. They want Canada to continue evolving as a country, as a nation state, and not as a loose collection of provinces. They turn to the federal government to protect our shared national interests and promote our nationality and our culture in times of peace and war.

Yet decentralization has proceeded at such an unchecked, disturbing rate that our federal government is at risk of becoming a hollow shell, so stripped of power as to be incapable of representing and guiding our country into a prosperous future.

This book addresses the rising threat of decentralization. It is hoped it will serve as a wake-up call for Canadians everywhere.
- **Michael B. Davie.**

"The demands for provincial legislative powers came mainly from the French Canadians, for whom the establishment of a Quebec legislature was the major attraction of Confederation."

- **Garth Stevenson**

CHAPTER ONE

THE MOVE TOWARDS DECENTRALIZATION

Exploring the rise
of provincial power

Sir John A. Macdonald's original 1867 vision was that of a highly-centralized Canada in which the federal government would provide nation-hood, control over most economic matters and control over provincial governments which would play a secondary role administering local concerns.

In his view, Ottawa should take full advantage of its British North America Act powers over trade and commerce, defence, banking, taxation, and other measures deemed necessary to provide for peace, order and good government, including using federally-appointed provincial lieutenant-governors to disallow provincial legislation at odds with Ottawa.   1.

Canada's first prime minister clearly envisioned a Canada shaped by centralization, defined as that which has the centre as its focus, in which the power and authority is concentrated in a central organization (in Macdonald's vision: the federal government) and which plays a dominant role over non-central organizations.   2.

This view was, of course, opposite to decentralization, defined as that which breaks up a concentration of governmental power at the centre and distributes it more widely.   3.

This book will show that, far from Sir John A Macdonald's preference for a clearly centralized federal nation, Canada has evolved into one of the most decentralized countries in the world.

As well, this paper will argue that, with the exception of a few brief and extraordinary, unifying moments in Canadian history, the ongoing shift towards decentralization has been virtually relentless.

Why Canada should find the force of decentralization so irresistible will be explored in this book, with particular regard to the decentralizing influences of Judicial Committee of the Privy Council in England and the JCPC-assisted growth in power of provincial governments.

First, it should be understood that Confederation itself , the uniting of the four former colonies of Canada West (Ontario), Canada East (Quebec), New Brunswick and Nova Scotia; and the initial centralist thrust of this union were to some degree, part of a unifyied response to a perceived take-over threat from the United States in the 1860s, following the American Civil War. As R. Douglas Francis, Richard Jones and Donald B. Smith state:

> "Fear of an American take-over during the Civil War was perhaps the leading cause of Canadian confederation." 4.

Craig Brown notes that the American threat also provided some of the thrust for the post-Confederation National Policy to unite the provinces through a national railway which would open up the riches of the West and through tariffs which would secure the domestic market for Canadian companies while heading off American competition. As Brown notes:

> "The United States played an interesting role in the National Policy that emphasized its nationalistic assumptions. Fundamental to the thinking of the framers of the policy was the idea that the United States was ... an aggressive competitor power waiting for a suitable opportunity to fulfil its destiny of the complete conquest of North America. The National Policy was intended to be the first line of defence against American ambitions." 5.

That Confederation also ended a political dead-
lock between the previously united Canadas is an
indication that even pre-Confederation there
existed jurisdictional tensions between former
colonies and their unified government.   6.

Yet, initially, the federal government 's centralist thrust attracted many of the politically elite.
As Roger Gibbons observes:

> "In the early years after Confederation, the
> centralized federal system put into place by
> the Constitution Act of 1867 was reinforced
> by a massive migration of political talent to
> Ottawa. With the exception of Ontario's
> Oliver Mowat, whowent on to become the
> province's premier, all the politicians voting
> for Confederation opted for elected or
> appointed national office. For the political
> movers and shakers, the action was in Ottawa
> and not in the provinces."   7.

Soon after Confederation, a new jurisdictional
debate began to rage over the extent of power
which ought to be accorded to the federal
government and provincial governments.

The weight behind centralist and decentralist
arguments depended very much on how the British
North America Act was interpreted - and which
side was doing the interpreting. Capturing the
essence of the centralist cause, Francis, Jones and
Smith observe:

> "Those who believe in the wide-ranging
> authority of the central government
> point out that the BNA Act delegated

18

precise and very circumscribed powers
to the provincial governments ... Central
ists contend the phrase "Peace, order
and good government of Canada," and
the phrase "regulation of trade and
commerce, " incorporated all powers not
exclusively given to the provinces, and
therefore the residuum of powers lies
with the federal government.

> Furthermore, the lieutenant governors of
> the provinces (all of whom were
> appointees of the dominion government)
> held the right to reserve and disallow
> provincial legislation."   8.

Yet, as Francis, Jones and Smith also note,
supporters of decentralization have been able to put
forth compelling arguments of their own:

> "Advocates of provincial rights argue, in
> contrast, that as the colonial
> leaders themselves established the union,
> Confederation is a compact made between
> political jurisdictions. They also point to the
> general phrase "property and civil rights in
> the province," in section 92 or the BNA Act
> which deals with the constitutional rights of
> the provinces, as proof of the intent to give
> broad powers to the provinces. Furthermore,
> they note provinces were given a structure of
> government similar to that of the federal
> government, implying that provinces have an
> association with the Crown similar, not
> subordinate, to that of the dominion."   9.

Macdonald's National policy and its inherent promise of opening up the western region of Canada to the business interests of central Canada helped draw support from Ontario and Quebec for centralism in the early years of federalism.

Yet, it wasn't long before Ontario and Quebec joined the hinterland provinces in challenging Macdonald's centralist vision. In particular, Quebec's unease with joining a larger, predominantly English-speaking society would make itself known.

As R. I. Cheffins and P.A. Johnson notes Quebec has long been interested in assuming "ownership and control of their economy."   10.

Garth Stevenson similarly emphasizes the pivotal role Quebec has played in the advancement of provincial powers when he notes:

> "The demands for provincial legislative powers came mainly from the French Canadians, for whom the establishment of a Quebec legislature was the major attraction of Confederation. The powers which they demanded for that legislature were mainly related to social institutions, education, the family, and the legal system."   11.

Ontario too joined the province's push for decentralization early on.

Oliver Mowat, premier from 1872-1896, has been called the Father of Provincial Rights for his forceful efforts to expand Ontario's provincial boundaries, have lieutenant governors appointed by the provinces (thus ending direct control by the federal government and the threat of disallowance of provincial legislation) and other legal rights.   12.

The cry for provincial powers was also heard in the west where the new provinces of Manitoba, Saskatchewan and Alberta were deprived by the federal government of jurisdiction over natural resources despite the fact that the other provinces had these rights. It wasn't until 1930 that the western provinces were made equal to the others - and therefore more powerful than they had previously been - following decades of alienation and demands for fair treatment.   13.

A dregree of decentralization was the natural outcome of providing western provinces with the same powers accorded the other provinces.

As well, the Maritimes sought and received additional provincial powers to prevent them from becoming small and irrelevant parts of a much greater whole. In many ways, the provinces' push for decentralization arrived with the dawn of Confederation and simply gained momentum following 1867.

Opposition to Macdonald's version of a centralized federal system was vociferous from the former colonies turned provinces.

Francis, Jones and Smith note that "the Maritimes, Quebec, and in Ontario, the Clear Grits, had resisted at the time of Confederation the idea legislative union, or highly centralized government with very weak local governments." 14.

They add:
"Macdonald's Conservative government maintained that major power should reside in the federal government. In contrast, the provincial premiers (most often Liberals) argued that the provinces were the main source of power and that they had voluntarily delegated only a portion of it to a central government..." 15.

As if this united front for decentralization was not enough, the provinces had a powerful judicial body to turn to which was sympathetic to their calls for more power.

Francis, Jones and Smith observe provincial governments bent on decentralization had a powerful ally in the JCPC:
"The Judicial Committee of the Privy Council, the highest court in the British Empire, consistently in the late nine teenth and early twentieth centuries interpreted the constitution in favour of the provinces. This constitutional court believed that the BNA Act gave wide powers to the provinces." 16.

Macdonald was to find that "the Judicial Committee's decisions were to play a decisive part in undermining his plans for a highly centralized federation." 17.

Through a number of provincial appeals, the JCPC came to enhance provincial powers at the expense of the federal government.

Whatever the driving force behind the JCPC's decisions, there was no mistaking the pro-provincial outcomes of landmark cases such as Hodge Vs the Queen in which the JCPC ruled provinces had the power to regulate liquor traffic within their boundaries and struck down a federal statute to issue liquor licences.

All of these pro-provincial rights JCPC rulings were to have a profound and lasting impact on the shift towards decentralization of Canada at the expense of the federal government and its preference for centralism.

Stevenson suggests the JCPC, led by Scottish Conservatives such as Lord Watson, may have applied the perspective of "a minority nation within a unity state," to the provinces to "maximize their powers in relation to the federal government." 18.

There were also the JCPC cases decided by Lord Watson that established the provinces as

governments equal to the federal government.
And there were the cases decided by Watson's
successor and fellow Scotsman Viscount Haldane
who struck down an array of federal legislation
regarding everything from regulations for the
insurance industry to an 18-year-old federal law to
deal with labor disputes.   19.

But the overall affect was to simply take many
powers away from the federal government. As
Stevenson observes:
> "Appeals were not, in fact, abolished until
> 1949, with the result that for almost a cen-
> tury the most influential concepts of Cana
> dian federalism were mainly defined by men
> who had no practical knowledge of Canada
> or of federalism, and who were not even
> required to live in that country. The Supreme
> Court of Canada ... increasingly deferred to
> the doctrines laid down by the JCPC."   20.

Thus far, we have seen that the shift towards
decentralization came about by the relentless
efforts of provinces to expand recognition of their
powers and that the decentralizing thrust was aided
in no small way by a number of key rulings by the
JCPC.

The JCPC was given a statutory basis by
the Imperial Parliament in Britain to rule on
jurisdictional disputes between the federal and
provincial governments in Canada - generally

on the basis of appeals from the provinces for greater powers.

As Garth Stevenson notes, there were other factors driving decentralization, including the lessening of the perceived take-over threat from the U.S. which had initially provided a common crisis to unify Canada under a centralist banner.

Alan Cairns has found that, in retrospect, the forces aiding decentralization were irresistible and Canada's evolution into a more decentralized federal state has been inevitable:

> "From the vantage point of a century of constitutional evolution, the centralist emphasis of the Confederation settlement appears increasingly unrealistic .... in the long run centralization was inappropriate for the regional diversities of a land of vast extent and a large, geographically concentrated, minority culture ..."   21.

He adds: "The existence of Quebec alone has been sufficient to prevent Canada from following the centralist route..."   22.

Indeed, it's possible that JCPC's pro-province judicial interpretations actually performed, to some degree, the helpful function of easing regional pressures from Quebec which might have become explosive.

Former Prime Minister Pierre Trudeau says:
"It has long been a custom in English
Canada to denounce the Privy Council for its
provincial bias; but it should perhaps be con
sidered that if the law lords had not leaned in
that direction, Quebec separation might not be
a threat today: it might be an accomplished
fact." 23.

Another factor behind the shift to decentralization has been the general tendency for many of
Macdonald's successors to be less interested in a
firmly centralized federal system and more interested in harmonious federal-provincial relations.

Macdonald's immediate successor, Sir Wilfrid
Laurier, was the first prime minister to accept
what would fast develop into a trend towards
greater decentralization. His openness to greater
provincial independence, at a time of relative
prosperity, brought in a co-operative era in the
1890s. Richard Simeon and Ian Robinson note:
"The economic successes of the wheat
boom, corresponding roughly with the
Laurier era, might have strengthened
federal legitimacy and, with it,
Macdonald's centralized quasi-federal
ideals. But under Laurier, the federation
had already decentralized considerably ...
the principal moral was that political
decentralization and economic growth
were compatible." 24.

As well, partisan rivalry between Liberal provinces and the Conservative federal government fueled decentralization. So did the unforeseen powers that control over natural resources would give the provinces in the building of highways and hydro-electrical projects.

Also fuelling decentralization was the addition of new provinces and premiers to further outnumber the federal government.

Another factor prompting decentralization was the ongoing tendency to indulge in province-building, particularly Quebec which has continually sought greater provincial powers as a means of protecting its French Fact from assimilation into the rest of Canada.

Yet, just as Macdonald was able to rely on the perceived threat of war with the United States in the 1860s to achieve an initially centralist federal system, another national crisis, the First World War, would also aid in interrupting the decentralizing evolution of Canada.

Gibbons notes the war united English Canadians in a "collective national endeavour and, not coincidentally, ushered in a sustained period of national dominance within the federal system." 25.

However, Quebec's anti-conscription stance isolated that province while the other provinces simply put their differences and bids for more political power on hold during the war.

Once the war ended, the provinces quickly resumed their efforts to enhance their powers, introducing gasoline taxes and a variety of commercial licensing fees which added enormously to their ability to increase their wealth.

By the time the 1930s Great Depression hit, most provinces had achieved an historically high degree of independence, relying on the federal government for only 13 per cent of their revenues.

As Simeon and Robinson assert, "by 1929, a decentralized version of the classical model of federalism was firmly in place - sociologically, politically and constitutionally." 26.

The Great Depression provided another crisis which united Canadians in the common cause although the federal government took a cautious approach, possibly in deference to Quebec which argued strongly for increased decentralization to better enable the provincial government to deal with the depression.

Simeon and Robinson observe that "the federal government did not implement reforms on a scale equivalent to those of Roosevelt's New Deal - nor did Canadian federalism undergo the same process of centralization." 27.

The Second World War also united Canadians in the face of a common crisis and enhanced the federal government's powers as the central government began to play a far more expanded role in enlarging the welfare state to accommodate farm supplement and other social programs during the war-generated economic boom and virtual full employment.   28.

In the aftermath of the war, there was a political price to pay for going against Quebec's anti-conscription position. As Simeon and Robinson assert:

> "... the Second World War exacerbated French-English conflicts, as had the First. It did not cost (Prime Minister Mackenzie) King power in Ottawa ... but it cost him the Liberal government of Quebec and, with it, any hope of dealing with a Quebec government open to centralizing constitutional ammendments."   29.

Richard Simeon notes that "the presence of Quebec, the preoccupation of the federal government with national unity in the face of a still regionalized society, and the difficulties of achieving constitutional change all meant that the federal framework remained intact - centralization proceeded less far in Canada than in a number of other countries."   30.

As F. R. Scott observes, "the advent of war in 1939 brought the "emergency" doctrine into play. Instantly provincial autonomy gave way, to the extent considered necessary by Ottawa to overcome the emergency."   31.

From 1945 through to about 1965, the 20-year , post-war period was also one of co-operative federalism in which the provinces continued to grow in strength as they were the administrators of numerous programs jointly financed by federal and provincial governments. This would mark perhaps the longest period in Canadian history of relative dominance by the federal government over the provinces.   32.

Central to this period was the post-war Keynesian Compromise based on the fiscal principles set out by the economist Keynes who advocated a central role for the state in spending - with deficits if necessary - during hard times, then building up surpluses during good times.

This era was also marked by a shift to continentalism, a closer integration of Canadian and American economies.
All of this put the federal government in the commanding position of being able to use its income tax spending powers to get involved in numerous social programs.   33.

By 1957, John Diefenbaker's Progressive Conservative government was advocating a pan-Canadian approach based on the concept of one nation and a blurring of provincial identities and disparities through national programs and equalization grants.   34.

But in the late 1960s, the Keynesian Compromise had been discredited through stagflation, the combination of high unemployment, high inflation and a stagnant economy.   35.

All of this left Prime Minister Pierre Trudeau struggling to retain a dominant role for the federal government through the imposition of several national programs.

Acting on another potentially-unifying crisis - the Energy Crisis of oil cartels and rapidly rising prices - Trudeau substantial federal power over the economy and the provinces through such measures as wage and price controls, the Foreign Investment Review Agency to screen corporate take-overs and the National Energy Program which took control of Alberta oil prices, driving them downwards for the benefit of eastern business and consumers. 36.

However, Trudeau's centralist approach was overturned by the Brian Mulroney Progressive Conservative government of the 1980s through early 1990s.

Mulroney replaced FIRA with Investment Canada which greatly reduced federal government control over foreign investment.

He also abandoned the controlled economy approach of Trudeau for the free market, perhaps best-illustrated by his government's hands-off approach to the economy and natural resources and the Canada-United States Free Trade Agreement which reduced the federal government's ability to intervene in the economy through subsidies or buy-Canadian policies.

In addition, Mulroney attempted – but failed - to enact two different constitutional accords - Meech Lake and Charlottetown - which would have succeeded in further decentralizing federal power to the provinces while recognizing Quebec as a distinct society.

Indeed, the Mulroney drift towards decentralization has been remarkable. As Janine Brody observes:

> "The drama of politics in the past decade is, in many ways, a chronicle of how the Conserva tive party succeeded in forging new regional alliances in order to displace the Liberals and thereby realize their version of a decentralized, continentalist, market-driven economy." 37.

Quebec in particular has taken to exerting previously unseen provincial power. For example,

the province's decision to invoke the notwithstanding clause in the Charter of Rights in order to overturn the ruling of the Supreme Court of Canada that Quebec's Law 101 prohibiting the use of English on exterior store signs was an unconstitutional violation of the basic human right of freedom of expression. 38.

Indeed, Quebec continues to issue bids for the powers which would virtually establish it as a separate entity altogether.

Ryszard Cholewinkski is among a number of political observers who anticipate the 1990s will yet see the "emergence of a new arrangement between Quebec and the rest of Canada ...based in some way on sovereignty-association." 39.

Meanwhile, Donald Smiley contends that the Mulroney government's steady drift towards decentralization has left the federal government weak and without a central focus:
"The price of such change ... has been a profound absence of national direction. Without such direction and without any coherent national vision articulated by the leadership of the federal parties, Canadian politics becomes little more than a 'scuffle of private interests'." 40.

Richard Simeon says the federal government is increasingly finding it lacks sufficient powers to be fully effective on the international stage.

Simeon notes the federal government's power is "draining on the one hand to supra-national institutions and one the other to smaller local institutions (provinces) - the main federal levers have become more and more constrained." 41.

It appears likely that the provincial forays into international affairs and trade will increase in coming years.

As Grant Reuber observes the provinces are working counter to the need for a strong federal government voice in international markets. He asserts: "all signs point to a substantial decentralization of power from Ottawa to the provinces." 42.

From all of this, Canada can be seen as a federal nation which began with a strongly centralized vision but soon came to embark on a pronounced trend towards increased decentralization.

The decentralization trend was relatively constant, incurring interruptions during times of national crisis when the provinces would put their decentralizationist demands on hold for the duration of the emergency and, in the case of World War II, for an extended recovery period following the emergency.

However, we've also seen that in the absence of a unifying crisis or in the presence of a perceived federal failure such as the collapse of the Keynesian Compromise, the provinces' push for decentralization intensifies and that some degree of province-building still occurs even during those moments when the federal government manages to borrow centre stage.

The mere existence of provinces has been enough to ensure some degree of decentralist province-building efforts will take place.

This reality is further sharpened by the presence of two very large provinces: Ontario, an economic giant; and Quebec, a predominantly French-speaking jurisdiction with many features of nation state an entrenched practice of pushing for greater powers to protect its distinct culture and set itself apart from the rest of Canada.

Garth Stevenson agrees with this bleak outlook for further decentralization, asserting that the degree to which Canada has already decentralized is unhealthy:

"...the picture that Canada presents to the outside world is that of an increasingly loose collection of semi-sovereign provinces, with a central government unable or unwilling to exercise much control over the economy or to carry out coherent policies even within its own fields of jurisdiction. Compared with almost any other modern state, or with Canada itself as recently as the 1950s, the extent of provin cial power and the passivity of the central government are remarkable." 43.

As Stevenson concludes, Canada is today in a weakened position due to decentralization and a reversal of this trend may be needed to restore effectiveness to the nation's ability to function in the world:

> "Canada is a relatively small, industrialized country in a world where most of its competitors are larger, stronger, and more centralized. If it is to survive in this environment and to overcome the divisive effects of its geographical barriers and its closeness to the United States, it may require a stronger central government that it has enjoyed in recent years and a corresponding reduction in the powers of provincial governments." 44.

Aided by landmark JCPC rulings and their own efforts, the provinces have achieved a degree of decentralization that I, and many political observers cited in this book, consider to be unhealthy for the viability of Canada as an independent nation state.

Given that Canada is today one of the most decentralized countries in the world, it remains to be seen if future Canadian federal governments will demonstrate the desire, the will and the capacity to reverse the decentralization trend - before it's too late for everyone who loves this country.

End Notes

For Chapter One

1. Kenneth McNaught, The Penguin His
   tory of Canada, (Markham: Penguin
   Books Canada Ltd., 1988), pp. 134-136.

2. Webster's New World Dictionary, David
   B. Guralnik, Editor in Chief, (New
   York: Simon and Schuster Inc., 1984),
   p. 231.

3. IBID, p. 365.

4. R. Douglas Francis, Richard Jones &
   Donald B. Smith, Origins. Canadian
   History To Confederation, (Toronto:
   Holt, Rinehart & Winston Canada,
   1988), p. 378.

5. Craig Brown, 'The Nationalism of
   the National Policy,' from Readings in
   Canadian History. Post-Confederation,
   edited by R. Douglas Francis & Donald
   B. Smith, (Toronto: Holt, Rinehart and
   Winston, 1990), p. 39.

6. R. Douglas Francis & Donald B. Smith, Readings in Canadian History. Pre-Confederation, (Toronto: Holt, Rinehart and Winston, 1990), p. 504.

7. Roger Gibbons, Conflict & Unity, (Toronto: Nelson, 1990), p. 224.

8. R. Douglas Francis, Richard Jones & Donald B. Smith, Destinies. Canadian History Since Confederation, (Toronto: Holt, Rinehart and Winston of Canada Ltd., 1988), pp. 7-8.

9. IBID, p. 8.

10. R. I. Cheffins & P.A. Johnson, The Revised Canadian Constitution, (Toronto: McGraw-Hill Ryerson Ltd., 1986), p. 119

11. Garth Stevenson, Unfulfilled Union: Canadian Federalism and National Unity, (Toronto: Gage Educational Publishing Company, 1989), p. 29. (Toronto: Gage Educational Publishing Company, 1989), p. 47.

21. Alan C. Cairns, 'The Judicial Committee and Its Critics,' from Federalism in Canada. Selected Readings, edited by Garth Stevenson, (Toronto: McClelland & Stewart Inc., 1989), pp. 94-96.

12. R. Douglas Francis, Richard Jones & Donald B. Smith, Destinies. Canadian History Since Confederation, (Toronto: Holt, Rinehart and Winston of Canada, 1988), pp. 64-67.

13. J. Peter Meekison, 'The Amending Formula,' from Perspectives on Canadian Federalism, edited by R. D. Olling & M. W. Westmacott, (Scarborough: Prentice Hall, 1988), p. 68.

14. R. Douglas Francis, Richard Jones & Donald B. Smith, Destinies. Canadian History Since Confederation, (Toronto: Holt, Rinehart and Winston of Canada, 1988), p. 64.

15. IBID.

16. IBID, p. 8.

17. Garth Stevenson, Unfulfilled Union. Canadian Federalism and National Unity, (Toronto: Gage Educational Publishing Company, 1989), pp. 46-47.

18. IBID, p. 49.

19. IBID, pp. 49-53.

20. Garth Stevenson, Unfulfilled Union. Canadian Federalism and National Unity,

22. IBID, p. 95.

23. Pierre Elliott Trudeau, Federalism And The French Canadians, (Toronto: The Macmillan Company of Canada Ltd., 1968), p. 198.

24. Richard Simeon and Ian Robinson, State, Society, and the Development of Canadian Federalism, (Toronto: University of Toronto Press, 1990) pp. 56.

25. Roger Gibbons, Conflict & Unity, (Scarborough: Nelson, 1990), p.225.

26. Richard Simeon and Ian Robinson, State, Society, and the Development of Canadian Federalism, (Toronto: University of Toronto Press, 1990), p. 56.

27. IBID, p. 61.

28. IBID, p. 90.

29. Richard Simeon and Ian Robinson, State, Society, and the Development of Canadian Federalism, (Toronto: University of Toronto Press, 1990), p. 90.

30. Richard Simeon, 'Considerations on Centralization and Decentralization', from Perspectives on Canadian Federalism, edited by R. D. Olling and M. W. Westmacott, (Scarborough: Prentice-Hall Canada Inc., 1988), p. 370.

31. F. R. Scott, 'Centralization and Decentralization in Canadian Federalism,' from Federalism in Canada, edited by Garth Stevenson, (Toronto: McClelland & Stewart Inc., 1989), p. 70.

32. Harold D. Clarke, Jane Jenson, Lawrence Le Duc & Jon H. Pammett, Absent Mandate, (Toronto: Gage Educational Publishing Company, 1991), pp. 14-16.

33. IBID.

34. IBID.

35. IBID

36. Richard Simeon, 'Considerations on Centralization and Decentralization', from Perspectives on Canadian Federalism, edited by R. D. Olling and M. W. Westmacott, (Scarborough: Prentice-Hall Canada, 1988), pp 370-374.

37. Janine Brodie, 'Tensions from Within: Regionalism and Party Politics in Canada', from Party Politics in Canada 6th Edition, edited by Hugh G. Thorburn, (Scarborough: Prentice-Hall Canada, 1991), p. 231.

38. Reg Whitaker, 'The Overriding Right,' from Canadian Politics 91/92, edited by Gregory S. Mahler and Roman R. March, (Guilford, Conn.: Dushkin Publishing Group, 1991), p. 37.

39. Richard I. Cholewinski, Human Rights In Canada: Into the 1990s and Beyond, (Ottawa: Human Rights Research and Education Centre, 1990), p. 122.

40. Donald V. Smiley, The Federal Condition In Canada, (Toronto: McGrawHill Ryerson Ltd., 1987), p. 187.

41. Richard Simeon, 'Concluding Comments,' from Canadian Federalism: Meeting Global Economic Challenges?' edited by Douglas M. Brown and Murray G. Smith, (Kingston: Queen's University, 1991), p. 287.

42. Grant L. Reuber, 'Federalism and Negative-Sum Games' from Coederation In Crisis, edited by Robert Young, (Toronto: James Lorimer & Company, 1991), p. 543.

43. Garth Stevenson, 'Federalism and Intergovernmental Relations,' from Canadian Politics in the 1990s, 3rd Edition, edited: Michael S. Whittington and Glen Williams, (Toronto: Nelson Canada, 1990), pp. 397-398.

44. IBID, p. 399.

Active ingredient?

Did the Judicial Committee of the Privy Council save the Canadian Federation?

Or, did the JCPC allow, even encourage, a destructive decentralization trend that continues to this day?

In the following mid-1990s essay, prepared for Political Science professor Dr. Janet Ajzenstat, I argued that the JCPC played a major role in stripping the federal govenrment of many of its powers. I further argued that this denuding of federal power has left our national government in a weakened state that ultimately places our country at risk.

CHAPTER TWO

The Judicial Committee
of the Privy Council:
The active ingredient in the early decentralization of Canada

Did the Judicial Committee of the Privy Council save the Canadian Federation?

Former Prime Minister Pierre Trudeau is among those who are inclined to answer this question in the affirmative.

Trudeau has indicated that the JCPC kept the federation sound by accommodating powerful pressure from the provinces for more powers.

In essence, Trudeau concludes, the JCPC stopped these pressures from reaching a destructive boiling point by making a number of rulings which had the decentralizing effect of building up provincial powers while diminishing federal powers.

Trudeau suggests that if not for the JCPC, Quebec demands for power might have become explosive. As he points out:

> "It has long been a custom in English Canada to denounce the Privy Council for its provincial bias; but it should perhaps be considered that if the law lords had not leaned in that direction, Quebec separation might not be a threat today: it might be an accomplished fact." 1

Alan Cairns has asserted that it is unrealistic to blame the decentralization of Canada on the JCPC.

Cairns suggests powerful provincial forces driving decentralization were irresistible and Canada's evolution into a more decentralized federal state has been inevitable:

> "From the vantage point of a century of constitutional evolution, the centralist emphasis of the Confederation settlement appears increasingly unrealistic .... in the long run centralization was inappropriate for the regional diversities of a land of vast extent and a large, geographically concentrated, minority culture ... The existence of Quebec alone has been sufficient to prevent Canada from following the centralist route..." 2.

But Cairns - and I - argue that decentralization was anything but inevitable, that provincial demands for more power did not have to be accommodated and that far from saving the Canadian federation, the JCPC actually hindered the nation's ability to respond to national concerns such as the Great Depression.

When added to power-seeking provinces, The JCPC served as the active ingredient in a virtual recipe for the legacy of excessive decentralization Canada is saddled with today.

That decentralization was not a natural outcome of Canadian evolution is clear from the text of the Constitution Act 1867 and from the pronouncements of the original framers.   3.

Although many of the 33 Fathers of Confederation were not entirely comfortable with the centralizing character of the Canadian union, there was no attempt to hide the degree of power given the federal government and it was an openly-centralist union which received sufficient support to come into being.   4.

Noting that "no intention of the Fathers of Confederation was more clear than that the new nation was to have a strong central government," Frank R. Scott observed that "in contrast to the American colonies, which approached union from the position of sovereign and independent states, and gave up their full powers with reluctance, the Canadian provinces came to union as colonies," and that "several opponents of Confederation based their opposition precisely on the ground that there was too much centralization.   5.

A measure of the centralist strength of the original federation was evident in disallowance powers (Sec. 56) which allowed the federal government to strike down provincial legislation within a year of passage.

The centralist thrust was also apparent in federal reservation powers which allowed federally-appointed lieutenant-governors of provinces to simply refuse to sign a provincial bill into law until it had been reviewed by federal cabinet which could strike down the bill.

Under reservation powers, federally-appointed lieutenant governors could refuse to approve a bill (although they wee likely acting on the federal government's behalf in any event).   6.

Concerning these powers, Peter Russell suggests "no element of the Constitution was potentially more threatening to provincial autonomy than federal powers powers of reservation and disallowance."   7.

Regarding Canada's origin as a highly-centralized country, K. C. Wheare suggests this feature means the Constitution Act, 1867 can best be described as a "quasi-federal constitution."   8.

However, while a majority of the Fathers of Confederation favoured a highly-centralized federa

Garth Stevenson notes that Oliver Mowat, decentralist Ontario premier of 1872-1896 and the leader of province-building undermined the centralist vision. As Peter Russell observes "the most effective constitutional force in the new federation was the provincial rights movement." 9.
Mowat, the "Father of Provincial Rights" found his province-building efforts rivalled by those in Quebec "for whom the establishment of a Quebec legislature was the major attraction of Confederation." 10.

As R. I. Cheffins and P.A. Johnson note Quebec has long been interested in assuming "ownership and control of their economy." 11.

A cry for provincial powers was also heard in the West where Manitoba, Alberta and Saskatchewan were deprived by the federal government of jurisdiction over natural resources until 1930 despite the fact that the other provinces had these rights. 12.

Although Sir John A. Macdonald had endeavoured to bring the Constitution Act 1867's centralist thrust to fruition, some of his successors proved more willing to live with decentralization and a weaker federal government in an effort to cultivate harmonious federal-provincial relations.

His immediate successor, Sir Wilfrid Laurier, was the first to accept a developing trend towards greater a greater degree of decentralization.

Richard Simeon and Ian Robinson suggest that Laurier's openness to greater provincial independence during a period of relative prosperity in the

1890s fostered "the principal moral that political decentralization and economic growth were compatible." 13.

Prior to Confederation, the JCPC, consisting of five judges drawn from the law lords of the House of Lords, served as final court of appeal for British colonies and it continued in this capacity under section 129 of the Constitution Act, 1867. 14.

F. L. Morton also affirms that the Constitution Act, 1867 "establishing a highly-centralized form of federalism," was subjected to interpretation by the JCPC and was "modified considerably by subsequent political developments in which judicial review played a major role." 15.

In the 16-year period of 1880-1896, the JCPC decided more than 75 per cent of 18 division of powers cases in favor of the provinces. 16.

Russell notes that "during the first thirty years of Confederation, the provinces made their most tangible constitutional gains not through the process of formal constitutional amendment but through litigation in the courts... in London before the Judicial Committee of the Privy Council." 17.

Most of the JCPC's rulings diminished federal powers inherent in the Peace, Order and Good Government and Trade and Commerce clauses of the Constitution Act 1867.

Acknowledging that the JCPC "played a major role in the constitutional development of Canada," Morton asserts that the cumulative impact of years of the JCPC's rulings regarding the federal division of powers "significantly diminished the authority of the federal government while expanding that of the prov inces." 18.

Morton further notes that the establishment of the Supreme Court of Canada in 1875 did not eliminate appeals to the JCPC.

In per saltum appeals, the courts of appeal in the provinces could appeal directly to the Privy Council.

This allowed parties to "effectively bypass the Supreme Court of Canada and reduced its prestige and influence." 19.

Nor did the issues of the day necessarily call out for increased provincial power at the expense of the weakened federal government.

Peter Russell notes:
> "In the 1870s when the practice of bringing constitutional challenges against legislation in favour... The Supreme Court judges gave the widest possible interpretation of the federal government's exclusive power to make laws in relation to 'the regulation of trade and com- merce', and supported this judgement by arguing that the Constitution's framers wished to avoid the evils of states rights that had plagued the American federation..." 20.

However, Russell also notes the centralist decisions by the Supreme Court were later reversed by the JCPC, effectively rendering the Supreme Court, "supreme in name only."   21.

An example of the Supreme Court's early centralist bent was evident in 1878 when the Court ruled in Severn v. The Queen that an Ontario act requiring federally-licensed liquor manufacturers to also acquire a provincial license to sell liquor wholesale was invalid on grounds that it was ultra vires. The provincial act was seen as intruding on federal trade and commerce powers and the Supreme Court was determined to protect the national powers of the federal government.   22.

However, the Court's centralist sympathies did not prevail against the decentralist JCPC which remained the ultimate court of appeal until 1949.

Morton suggests this left the Supreme Court of Canada "functionally more like a middle-tier British appeal court until 1949, and the habits and procedures associated with such a court lingered for another generation."   23.

Nor was the JCPC inclined to pay heed to the
 Morton notes that until 1949, the Court was "clearly the junior partner in overseeing the judicial centralist passages of the BNA Act. In Citizens Insurance Co. v. Parsons; Queen Insurance Co. v. Parsons, in 1881, the JCPC made another province-building decision when it upheld as intra vires the

Ontario Fire Insurance Policy Act.   Not only did the JCPC decision apply a further limitation to the exclusivity of federal trade and commerce powers, but as Russell, Knopff and Morton point out, "the Judicial Committee treated interpretation of the BNA Act no differently than it would treat the interpretation of an ordinary statute.   24.

No reference was made to the historical context in which the constitution was drafted nor to the intentions of the Fathers of Confederation."   25.

The case of Russell v. The Queen in 1882 marked an early and extremely rare instance when the JCPC actually found in favor of federal power over provincial power.

The JCPC found the Dominion's Temperance Act of the federal government was intra vires on grounds that it fell under the government's general, residuary 'peace, order and good government' powers.

Council's use of the peace, order and good government power in the Russell case as a constitutional basis for federal legislation proved to be highly exceptional as subsequent decisions considerably narrowed

In the 1892 case Liquidators of the Maritime Bank of Canada v. Receiver General of New Brunswick, Lord Watson flatly rejected the federal government's position that Confederation had eliminated direct ties between provinces and the Crown (which would thereby deny New Brunswick's tactic for becoming a secured creditor of a failed bank's assets) by making provinces subordinate to the federal government.

Lord Watson's decision avoided examining "in minute detail, the provisions of the Act of 1867," gave little credence to Macdonald's numerous public statements about the superior, central powers of the federal government, and made no mention at all of general federal powers or those of disallowance and reservation which quite clearly did put the provinces in a subordinate position to the federal government.

Instead, Lord Watson appeared to rely on A. V. Dicey's classical definition of federalism based on autonomous states, with little apparent regard for Macdonaldonian views that the BNA Act did not place Canada in the classical federal mode, but rather in a highly centralized variation of federalism. 25.

In the Local Prohibition Case of 1896, the JCPC reversed the Supreme Court's prior ruling that an Ontario prohibition law was unconstitutional and ultra vires because it intruded on federal jurisdiction over trade and commerce.

Lord Watson's ruling had the effect of further restricting the exclusivity of federal trade and commerce power.
After also finding that trade and commerce powers did not specifically apply in this case because trade was being banned, not regulated, Lord Watson asserted that the applicable powers under peace, order and good government did not prevent provinces from passing like legislation of their own, thus also diminishing exclusivity of POGG powers.
its scope."   26.

This case also marked a turning point for the Supreme Court of Canada which, having endured yet another reversal of its centralist pro-federal government rulings, began to interpret the Constitution in line with JCPC decentralist views.   27.

The JCPC continued to restrict federal general powers in the Board of Commerce and Combines and Fair Prices case of 1919, 1922. The JCPC by this point had diminished the federal government's general powers to essentially auxiliary power, inferior to other powers of federal and provincial governments.

The JCPC's Viscount Haldane struck down the federal legislation which was intended to stop post-war profiteering and monopolization of businesses.

Viscount Haldane also expressed the view that the federal government should only use criminal law power in areas of established criminal jurisprudence - and post-war profiteering did not fit this category. 28.

Perhaps the most striking example of the JCPC diminishing federal powers occurred in the Toronto Electric Commissioners v. Snider case in 1925.

The federal government had established in 1907 its Industrial Disputes Investigation Act which pro-vided for conciliation and arbitration in labor disputes involving economic sectors the federal government deemed vital to the nation, including mines, transpor-tation, communications and public service utilities.

After existing for almost 20 years, the Act was struck down by the JCPC after Viscount Haldane found that it did not meet his "emergency test" in which POGG powers were, in his unique interpretation, only to be used in national emergencies, despite the complete lack of such a restriction in the Constitution Act 1867.

Regarding Haldane's emergency doctrine, Russell, Knopff and Morton note that Haldane tried to reconcile his ruling with the Russell case by making "the least plausible, but perhaps most entertaining extension of this approach," when he suggested that the Canada Temperance Act was upheld by the JCPC because the Privy Council must have regarded drunkenness as a national menace.

Haldane suggested that drunkenness must have been "so serious and pressing that the National Parliament was called on to intervene to protect the nation from disaster - an epidemic of pestilence might conceivably have been regarded as analogous."   29.

Even when the JCPC occasionally ruled in the federal government's favor, the ruling could still have the indirect effect of diminishing central powers such as trade and commerce.
An example of this occurred in the Proprietary Articles Trade Association case in 1931 in which the JCPC upheld the Supreme Court's unanimous finding that federal anti-combines legislation was intra vires and valid.

However, the JCPC rejected the Court's finding that the law was valid due to federal trade and com merce powers.

Instead, the JCPC upheld the law on narrower grounds that the legislation could be justified under criminal law and taxation powers.   30.

By 1932, Canada had been a sovereign country for 65 years and the JCPC appeared to recognize the nation's need for powers sufficient to implement national legislation when it upheld federal powers in the Aeronautics reference case.   Lord Sankey even went so far as to acknowledge that the real purpose of the B.N.A. Act was to give the central government the "almost sovereign powers," needed to pass laws on behalf of the whole country.   31.

That same year, the JCPC dealt directly with Canada's need for sufficient powers to implement international agreements when it upheld federal legislation in the Radio Case which was intended to allow the government to regulate radio communica-tions in the country.   32.

Unfortunately, the JCPC's reasoned response to national needs regarding the regulation of aeronautics and radio communications would be overshadowed by its striking down of most of Prime Minister R. B. Bennett's Depression era 'New Deal' legislation in 1937.   Bennett may been given a false sense of hope after the radio and aeronautics cases rulings but the JCPC passed little of his New Deal legislation beyond lesser legislation regulating depressed agricultural markets.   33.

All told, the JCPC struck down five of Bennett's eight social program pieces of legislation, including the unemployment insurance program in the Bennett government's Employment and Social Insurance Act of 1935, after the Act was challenged as ultra vires by the Liberal opposition under Mackenzie King.

When the Supreme Court of Canada upheld the legislation, King appealed the case to the JCPC and Lord Atkin who did not find that the Great Depression ravaging Canada constituted a national emergency and he rejected the notion that an unemployment insurance scheme was a proper use of federal spending powers in the provinces.

Russell, Knopff and Morton noted "the Privy Council's decisions in these cases were a grave disappointment to those in Canada who had hoped that the powers assigned by the constitution to the central government would be sufficiently broad to enable it to deal effectively with the nation-wide consequence of a severe economic depression." 34.

The JCPC's striking down of the Bennett 'New Deal 'legislation provoked an angry reaction from federal politicians, culminating in the O'Connor Report (1939) to the Senate, which advocated abolition of appeals to the JCPC.

The O'Connor Report argued that questions of Canadian constitutional law could be "better answered by Canadian judges, judges with first-hand familiarity with the political and economic realities of Canadian life." Appeals to the JCPC would be abolished in the late 1940s. 35.

58

Frank R. Scott has denounced the JCPC for severely undermining Canada's ability to respond to the national emergency of the Great Depression of the 1930s, for weakening the federal government and for being "too handicapped by its ignorance of Canada to be able to give good judgements in Canadian constitutional law." 36.

Supreme Court judge Bora Laskin has also argued that the JCPC were "uninformed and unnourished by any facts of Canadian living," resulting in decisions which limited Canada's ability to solve interprovincial problems and diminished the sense of Canadian nationality. 37.

Yet another diminution of federal power occurred in the Labour Conventions Case in which the JCPC struck down as ultra vires, depression era federal legislation designed to establish minimum wages, hours of work and paid days of rest under the draft conventions of the International Labour Organization that Canada had joined after World War I.

Lord Atkin found that although Canada had signed the Treaty of Versailles it was not obligated to then sign the labour conventions and having done so on its own, did not win the right to "invade" provincial jurisdiction.

Russell, Knopff and Morton say this JCPC ruling "dealt a lethal blow to the doctrine that the national Parliament had a plenary power of implementing treaties." 38.

They add that the decision greatly limited Canadian sovereignty in enacting international treaties:

> "The federal legislation emerged from this decision subject to much more severe limitations on its power of performing international obligations than the federal governments of the United States or Australia impose on their central legislature. Lord Atkin's approach in essence rendered the power of enforcing treaties thoroughly subject to the general division of powers in Canadian federalism. In effect this means that Canada cannot become a party to an international agreement which requires legislative action beyond the ambit of section 91 unless the prior approval of the provinces is first secure." 39.

F. L. Morton notes that Lord Atkin's decision was "widely perceived as a serious blow to the effective conduct of Canadian foreign policy, and was blamed on Lord Atkin's 'watertight compartments' view of Canadian federalism.

This view was widely condemned as being out of touch with the economic and political realities of twentieth-century Canada." 40.

Morton adds that the Privy Council's decision in the Labour Conventions Case was "only one in a series of constitutional cases that progressively narrowed the scope of the federal government's section 91 powers while expanding the section 92 jurisdiction of the provinces." 41.

He adds:

> "The federal government's broad residual
> power to make laws for the 'peace, order and
> good government of Canada' was whittled
> away to almost nothing by the Privy Council's
> 'emergency doctrine' test. The unrestricted
> power to make laws for the 'regulation of
> trade and commerce' was soon reduced to the
> narrower ambit of international and interpro-
> vincial trade' by judicial interpretation. At the
> same time, the JCPC's decisions expanded
> what originally appeared to be the rather
> meagre provincial powers to make laws in
> relation to 'property and civil rights in the
> province' and 'all matters of a merely local or
> private nature in the province'."   42.

The JCPC's last case in Canada was one initiated
by all three federal political parties in 1947 - but
opposed by the provinces: the abolition of appeals
from Canada to the JCPC which was followed by an
amendment in 1949 making the Supreme Court of
Canada the ultimate court of appeal.   43.

As Russell, Knopff and Morton observe, many
felt the changes were long overdue:

> "The antagonism aroused amongst English
> Canada's political and legal elite by the Privy
> Council's interpretation of the BNA Act,
> especially its decisions on the New Deal
> legislation, further fueled the fires of judicial
> nationalism. However, this factor was not

publicly acknowledged as a reason for
abolition by federal political leaders as they
did not wish to arouse provincial sensitivities
by implying that they hoped the Supreme
Court of Canada would adopt a more centralist
approach to constitutional interpretation." 44.

The JCPC rulings had the cumulative impact of
significantly undermining federal power. Russell,
Rainer Knopff and Ted Morton recount that, "in a
series of cases the Privy Council evolved a number of
implied limitations which had the effect of reducing
the federal commerce power in Canada to a pale
shadow of its counterpart in the United States Constitution." 45.

Cairns notes that English Canadian jurists unani-
mously condemned the provincial bias of JCPC decisions. Critics of the JCPC also condemned the Privy
Council for not following the centralist bias of the
constitution text closely enough. 46.

As Murray Greenwood notes, the Supreme Court's
centralist leanings were undone by a decentralist
JCPC which reversed "every major centralist doctrine
of the Court." 47.

Indeed, it is no accident that the greatest period of
centralization in Canada occurred in the 1950s
through early 1970s, a period immediately following
the 1949 abandonment of appeals to the JCPC.

As Christopher Manfredi notes, "the Supreme
Court began to fulfil the expectations of its centralist
supporters almost immediately after the abolition of
JCPC appeals." 48.

Prime Minister John Diefenbaker's Pan-Canadian approach, including his 1960 Canadian Bill of Rights, was eventually followed by Pierre Trudeau's centralist legislative measures including the National Energy Program regulating petroleum prices and Anti Inflation legislation limiting wages, as federal governments found the Supreme Court far more open to national legislative measures than the JCPC had ever been.

Morton notes that the Anti-Inflation reference case gave Supreme Court Justice Bora Laskin, "a known centralist and veteran critic of the JCPC, to repudiate once and for all the moribund 'emergency doctrine.' Several post-1945 decisions of the Supreme Court have silently ignored the old 'emergency doctrine' and spoke instead of 'an inherent national importance' test." 49.

Although the Supreme Court can point to a rough balance of numbers in its pro-federal and pro-provincial decisions, the provinces have complained that the decisions against them were far more important and damaging.
Edwin Black has denounced the federally-appointed judges as "sober grey men acting as spear-carriers for the federal prime minister..." 50.

F. L. Morton suggests that the power struggle between federal and provincial governments is natural and dates back to the dawn of Canada.
The federal ability to disallow provincial legislation was placed in the Constitution to help the

federal government prevail in such power struggles. Morton illustrates his point when he observes:

> "The Constitution Act, 1867, represented an uneasy compromise between these conflicting goals. Provincial demands for reserving localautonomy and self-government were accommodated through a distribution of legislative powers between the newly created federal government and the provinces, primarily in sections 91 and 92 of the Act. The centralists' goals were recognized by a very broad wording of the federal government's section 91 law-making powers, and by the unilateral power to strike down provincial laws through the devices of disallowance (section 56) and reservation (section 90).   50.

The power struggle between federal and provincial governments went to the very structure of the fledgling federation, with Ontario demanding that the lieutenant-governors represent the provinces – not the federal government, a clear shift in the mandate of the lieutenant-governors.   Peter Russell notes:

> "The first objective of the provincial rights movement was to resist and overcome a hierarchical version of Canadian federalism in which the provinces were to be treated as a subordinate or junior level of government. An early focal point of resistance was the office of provincial lieutenant-governor. From a Macdonald centralist perspective, the lieutenant-governors were essentially agents of the federal government in provincial capitals. In the 1870s, however, Ontario, under Mowat's

64

leadership began to insist that lieutenant-governors had full Crown powers in matters of provincial jurisdiction and that they exercised these powers on the advice of provincial ministers." 51

Russell also observes that the federal power of disallowance – even though Constitutionally enshrined – became virtually unusable. He points out:
"Over time, the principle of provincial autonomy - self-government in those areas constitutionally assigned to the provincial legislatures - became so strongly held in the Canadian political system that the federal powers of reservation and disallowance, though remaining in the Constitution, became politically unusable." 52.

Morton agrees disallowance remains a federal power in name only:
"The disallowance and reservation powers violate the principle of parity, and for that reason it has been argued that Canada is not a true federal state. However, neither power has been exercised by Ottawa for over 40 years. Although both powers exist legally, it is generally accepted that a convention of non-use has been established and that it is politically unacceptable for the federal government to reactivate either of these powers." 53.

From all of this, it is certainly safe to say that the Supreme Court, at the very least, rendered a number of decisions which were not seen as favoring the provinces and thus marked a departure from the JCPC legacy, a departure in which the Canadian federation has somehow survived intact without the JCPC being around to hand out new powers to the provinces at the federal government's expense.

Nor is there evidence to suggest that the JCPC's pro-provincial rights rulings have in any way satisfied Quebec. Canada survived the threat of Quebec separation under the Trudeau era but the decentralist era of Brian Mulroney witnessed more than the delegation of immigration powers to Quebec. It saw the rise of a virulent strain of separatism in which the Bloc Quebecois has become the Official Opposition and a referendum on 'sovereignty' would soon follow. Such referendums have been derided as "never-endums" as the separatist Quebec government will only accept a yes to separation and is intent on holding repeated referendums until it gets the answer it wants. So much for the people's democratic voice.

The lesson here is that JCPC-aided province-building has weakened the federal government without ending separation threats from Quebec.

Indeed, Quebec is now pointing to its enhanced powers as proof that it possesses the attributes of a nation state - and may therefore decide to officially become one.

Decentralization has not stopped Quebec from demanding far more powers.

Thanks in part to more than 70 years of meddling by the JCPC, Canada is today the most decentralized country in the world.

As Russell notes, "state governors in the United States, hemmed in by an elaborate system of checks and balances, are political pygmies compared with provincial premiers who perform as political giants on the national stage." 54.

Garth Stevenson presents a bleak outlook for further decentralization, asserting that "the picture that Canada presents to the outside world is that of an increasingly loose collection of semi-sovereign provinces, with a central government unable or unwilling to exercise much control over the economy or to carry out coherent policies even within its own fields of jurisdiction." 55.

Stevenson adds that:
"Canada is a relatively small, industrialized country in a world where most of its competitors are larger, stronger, and more centralized. If it is to survive in this environment and to overcome the divisive effects of its geographical barriers and its closeness to the United States, it may require a stronger central government than it has enjoyed in recent years and a corresponding reduction in the powers of provincial governments." 56.

The JCPC clearly performed the role of active ingredient in a recipe for province-building at the federal government's expense.

In saying yes to the provinces in most cases, the JCPC lent an air of legitimacy to provincial bids for more and more powers.

Whether the Scottish law lords sympathized with the provinces as being akin to little Scotlands struggling against a larger entity or whether they simply couldn't depart from their pre-Confederation role of adjudicating separate colonies, the result was the same: The substantial powers bestowed on Canada through the BNA Act were whittled down to a shadow of their former selves while provincial powers were steadily expanded.

As discussed, the JCPC's rulings had a damaging effect on Canada's ability to function as a sovereign nation.

The provision of direct appeals to the JCPC left the federal government and Supreme Court looking like superfluous layers of bureaucracy that could be easily side-stepped to approach the real power in Britain.

The severe limitations placed on Canada's ability to negotiate treaties or pass legislation to meet national needs served to weaken the nation's abiltity to function as legitimate state.

The sense of nationhood and national identity suffered as national programs were sacrificed to province-building.

The legitimacy of the federal government was undermined through JCPC decisions striking down federal law - even if in existence 18 years.

In striking down the Bennett 'New Deal' legislation, JCPC lords, who knew little of Canada or Canadian needs, interfered to prevent Canada from responding as nation to what was clearly a national emergency.

The JCPC delayed the implementation of the welfare state and hindered the national development of Canada.

From its centralist birth, Canada has devolved into a decentralized, weak state following decades of JCPC decisions diminishing federal powers. Far from saving the Canadian federation, the JCPC weakened Canada and undermined its ability to fully function as a nation.

End Notes

For Chapter Two

1. Pierre Elliott Trudeau, Federalism And The French Canadians, Toronto: The Macmillan Company of Canada Ltd., 1968, p. 198.

2. Alan C. Cairns, 'The Judicial Committee and Its Critics', from Federalism in Canada: Selected Readings, edited by Garth Stevenson, Toronto: McClelland & Stewart Inc., 1989, p. 95.

3. W. P. M. Kennedy, Essays in Constitutional Law, London: Oxford University Press, 1934, p. 83.

4. J. M. Beck, The Shaping of Canadian Federalism: Central Authority or Provincial Right?, Toronto: The Copp Clark Publishing Company, 1971, p. 7.

5. F. R. Scott, 'Political Nationalism and Confederation', Canadian Journal of Economics and Political Science, VIII , August, 1942, pp 399-400.

6. J. Peter Meekison, 'The Amending Formula', from Perspectives on Canadian Federalism, edited by R. D. Olling and M. W. Westmacott, Scarborough: Prentice Hall, 1988, p. 68.

7. Peter H. Russell, Constitutional Odyssey: Can Canadians Become a Sovereign People?, Toronto: University of Toronto Press, 1993, p 38.

8. K. C. Wheare, Federal Government, London: Oxford University Press, 1946, pp 19-20.

9. Peter H. Russell, Constitutional Odyssey: Can Canadians Become a Sovereign People?, Toronto: U. of Toronto Press, 1993, p. 34.

10. Garth Stevenson, Unfulfilled Union: Canadian Federalism and National Unity, Toronto: Gage Educational Publishing Company, 1989, p. 29.

11. R. I. Cheffins & P.A. Johnson, The Revised Canadian Constitution, Toronto: McGraw-Hill Ryerson Ltd., 1986, p. 19.

12. R. Douglas Francis, Richard Jones & Donald B. Smith, Destinies. Canadian History Since Confederation, Toronto: Holt, Rinehart and Winston of Canada, 1988, pp. 64-67.

13. Richard Simeon and Ian Robinson, State, Society, and the Development of Canadian Federalism, Toronto: University of Toronto Press, 1990, pp. 56-57.

14. F. L. Morton, Law, Politics and the Judicial Process in Canada, Second Edition, Calgary: University of Calgary Press, 1992, p 52.

15. Ibid, p. 339.

16. Peter H. Russell, Constitutional Odyssey: Can Canadians Become a Sovereign People?, Toronto: U. Press, 1993, p. 42.

17. Peter H. Russell, Constitutional Odyssey, Toronto: 1993, p. 40.

18. F. L. Morton, Law, Politics and the Judicial Process, Calgary: 1992, pp 52-53.

19. Ibid.

20. Peter H. Russell, Constitutional Odyssey, Toronto:, 1993, p. 41.

21. Ibid.

22. Severn v. The Queen, In the Supreme Court of Canada, 1878, 2. S.C.R. 70, as found in Peter H. Russell, Rainer Knopff and Ted Morton, Federalism and the Charter. Leading Constitu tional Decisions, Ottawa: Carleton University Press, 1993, p. 31.

23. F. L. Morton, Law, Politics and the Judicial Process, Calgary: 1992, p 341.

24. Citizens Insurance Co. v. Parsons; Queen Insur ance Co. v. Parsons, In the Privy Council, 1881, 7 app. Cas. 96; Olmstead 94, in Peter H. Russell, Rainer Knopff and Ted Morton, Feder alism and the Charter, Ottawa: 1993, pp. 37-49.

25. Russell v. The Queen, In the Privy Council, 1882, 7 App. Cas. 829; I Olmstead 145 in Peter H. Russell, et. al., Federalism and the Charter, Ottawa: 1993, pp. 43-48.

26. Liquidators of the Maritime Bank of Canada v. Receiver General of New Brunswick, In the Privy Council, 1892, A. C. 437; I Olmstead 263, in Peter H. Russell, et. al., Federalism and the Charter, Ottawa: 1993, pp. 50-52.

27. Attorney General of Ontario v. Attorney Gen
     eral of Canada, In the Privy Council, 1896, A.
     C. 348; I Olmstead 343, in Peter H. Russell, et.
     al., Federalism and the Charter, Ottawa: 1993,
     pp. 53-59.

28. In Re The Board of Commerce Act, 1919, and
     the Combines and Fair Prices Act, 1919, In the
     Privy Council, 1922, A. C. 191; II Olmstead
     245, in Peter H. Russell et. al., Federalism and
     the Charter, Ottawa: 1993, pp. 61-67.

29. Toronto Electric Commissioners v. Snider, In
     the Privy Council, 1925, A. C. 396; II Olmstead
     394, in Peter H. Russell, et al., Federalism and
     the Charter, Ottawa: 1993, pp. 73-77.

30. Proprietary Articles Trade Association v.
     Attorney General of Canada, 1931, In the Privy
     Council, 1931, A. C. 310; II Olmstead 668, in
     Peter H. Russell, et al., Federalism and the
     Charter, Ottawa: 1993, pp. 78-84.

31. In Re Regulation and Control of Aeronautics In
     Canada, In the Privy Council, 1932, A. C. 54; II
     Olmstead 709, in Peter H. Russell, et al., Feder
     alism and the Charter, Ottawa: 1993, pp. 85-92.

32. In Re Regulation and Control of Radio Com
     munications In Canada, In the Privy Council,
     1932, A. C. 304; III Olmstead 18, in Peter H.
     Russell, et al., Federalism and the Charter,
     Ottawa: 1993, pp. 93-96.

33. Attorney General of British Columbia v. Attor
     ney General of Canada, In the Privy Council,
     1937, A. C. 377; III Olmstead 228, in Peter H.
     Russell, et al., Federalism and the Charter,
     Ottawa: 1993, pp. 101-103.

34. Attorney General of Canada v. Attorney Gen
     eral of Ontario, In the Privy Council, 1937, A.
     C. 355; III Olmstead 207, in Peter H. Russell,
     et al., Federalism and the Charter, Ottawa:
     1993, pp. 97-100.

35. F. L. Morton, Law, Politics and the Judicial
     Process, Calgary: 1992, p 23.

36. Frank R. Scott, 'The Privy Council and Mr.
     Bennett's 'New Deal' Legislation', in F. R.
     Scott, Essays on the Constitution, Toronto:
     University of Toronto Press, p. 101.

37. Bora Laskin, 'Peace, Order and Good Govern
     ment re-examined', in Canadian Bar Review,
     25, 1947.

38. Attorney General of Canada v. Attorney Gen
     eral of Ontario (Labour Conventions Case), In
     the Privy Council, 1937, A.C. 327; III Olmstead
     180, in Peter H. Russell, et al., Federalism and
     the Charter, Ottawa: 1993, pp. 104-110.

39. Peter H. Russell, et al., Federalism and the
     Charter, Ottawa: 1993, p. 104.

40. F. L. Morton, Law, Politics and the Judicial
     Process, Calgary: 1992, p. 343.

41. Ibid.
42. Ibid.

43. Attorney General of Ontario v. Attorney Gen
     eral of Canada, In the Privy Council, 1947, A.
     C. 128; III Olmstead 508, in Peter H. Russell,
     et al., Federalism and the Charter, Ottawa:
     1993, pp. 122-129.

44.   Peter H. Russell, et al., Federalism and the
       Charter, Ottawa: 1993, p. 122.

45.   Peter H. Russell, Rainer Knopff & Ted Morton,
       Federalism and the Charter, Ottawa: 1993, p.31

46.   Alan C. Cairns, 'The Judicial Committee and its
       Critics,' in Canadian Journal of Political Sci
       ence, 4, September, 1971, p. 301.

47.   F. Murray Greenwood, 'Lord Watson, Institu
       tional Self-Interest and the Decentralization of
       Canadian Federalism in the 1890s', from Uni
       versity of British Columbia Law Review, 9,
       1974, p. 267.

48.   Christopher P. Manfredi, Judicial Power and the
       Charter, Toronto: McClelland & Stewart Inc.,
       1993, p. 30.

49.   F. L. Morton, Law, Politics and the Judicial
       Process, Calgary: 1992, p. 344.

50.   Edwin R. Black 'Supreme Court Judges as
       Spear-Carriers for Ottawa: They need Watch
       ing,' from Report on Confederation, February,
       1978, p. 12.

51.   Peter H. Russell, Constitutional Odyssey: Can
       Canadians Become a Sovereign People?,
       Toronto: University of Toronto Press, 1993, pp.
       37-38.

52.   Peter H. Russell, Constitutional Odyssey: Can
       Canadians Become a Sovereign People?,
       Toronto: University of Toronto Press, 1993, p.
       39.

53.   F. L. Morton, Law, Politics and the Judicial
      Process in Canada, Second Edition, Calgary:
      University of Calgary Press, 1992, p 340.

54.   Peter H. Russell, Constitutional Odyssey,
      Toronto: 1993, p. 36.

55.   Garth Stevenson, 'Federalism and Intergovern
      mental Relations,' from Canadian Politics in the
      1990s, Third Edition, edited by Michael S.
      Whittington and Glen Williams, Toronto:
      Nelson Canada, 1990, pp. 397-398.

56.   Ibid.

CASES CITED IN DETAIL:
(Listed in order of year heard)

1.   Severn v. The Queen, *In the Supreme Court of
Canada, 1878, 2. S.C.R. 70, in Russell, et. al,* Feder-
alism and the Charter, Ottawa: Carleton University
Press, 1993.

2.   Citizens Insurance Co. v. Parsons; Queen Insurance Co. v. Parsons, *In the Privy Council, 1881, 7
app. Cas. 96; Olmstead 94, in Russell, et. al.,* Federalism and the Charter, Ottawa: 1993.

3.   Russell v. The Queen, In the Privy Council, 1882,
7 App. Cas. 829; I Olmstead 145, in Russell, et. al.,
Federalism and the Charter, Ottawa: 1993.

4.   Liquidators of the Maritime Bank of Canada v. Receiver General of New Brunswick, *In the Privy Council, 1892, A. C. 437; I Olmstead 263, in Russell, et. al.,* Federalism and the Charter, Ottawa: 1993.

5.   Attorney General of Ontario v. Attorney General of Canada, *In the Privy Council, 1896, A. C. 348; I Olmstead 343, in Russell, et. al.,* Federalism and the Charter, 1993.

6.   In Re The Board of Commerce Act, 1919, and the Combines and Fair Prices Act, 1919, *In the Privy Council, 1922, A. C. 191; II Olmstead 245, in Russell, et. al.,* Federalism and the Charter, 1993.

7.   Toronto Electric Commissioners v. Snider, *In the Privy Council, 1925, A. C. 396; II   Olmstead 394, in Peter H. Russell, et al.,* Federalism and the Charter, 1993.

8.   Proprietary Articles Trade Association v. Attorney General of Canada, 1931, *In the Privy Council, 1931, A. C. 310; II Olmstead 668, in Russell, et al.,* Federalism and the Charter, 1993.

9.   In Re Regulation and Control of Aeronautics In Canada, *In the Privy Council, 1932, A. C. 54; II Olmstead 709, in Russell, et al.,* Federalism and the Charter, 1993.

10.   In Re Regulation and Control of Radio Communications In Canada, *In the Privy Council, 1932, A. C. 304; III Olmstead 18, in Russell, et al.,* Federalism and the Charter, 1993.

11.   Attorney General of British Columbia v. Attorney General of Canada, (Natural Products Marketing Act Reference), *In the Privy Council, 1937, A. C. 377; III Olmstead 228, in Russell, et al.,* Federalism and the Charter, 1993.

12.   Attorney General of Canada v. Attorney General of Ontario, *In the Privy Council, 1937, A. C. 355; III Olmstead 207, in Russell, et al.,* Federalism and the Charter, 1993.

13.   Attorney General of Canada v. Attorney General of Ontario (Labour Conventions Case), *In the Privy Council, 1937., A.C. 327; III Olmstead 180, in Russell, et al.,* Federalism and the Charter, 1993.

14.   Attorney General of Ontario v. Attorney General of Canada, (References re Abolition of Privy Council Appeals), *In the Privy Council, 1947, A. C. 128; III Olmstead 508 in Russell, et al.,* Federalism and the Charter, 1993.

CHAPTER THREE

Before and after The Charter:

Examining the protection of rights and the
Charter's impact on decentralization

The 1982 Canadian Charter of Rights and
Freedoms was warmly welcomed by Canadians who
saw within this historic document the comforting
cataloguing of the various rights and freedoms associated with the free and democratic society they live
in.

Here was a document which clearly set out the
array of limitations imposed on the state along with
well-defined and less-defined rights Canadians could
rely on.

Yet, life before the Charter was certainly not void of freedoms. Canadians had clearly enjoyed rights and freedoms long before these same rights and freedoms were officially recognized, described and listed within the Charter.

The pre-Charter experience raises two important questions to be addressed in this paper: Were Canadian rights and freedoms protected before the Charter came into existence? If so, were these rights well-protected?

I contend that through a body of common law, judicial precedents and accepted conventions, Canada had long enjoyed what can be aptly described as an unwritten charter of rights and freedoms, the recognition and spirit of which were at least partly manifested in the 1960 Canadian Bill of Rights which preceded the 1982 Charter.

As well, by referring to a number of cases both before and after the Charter, and by citing a number of constitutional experts - including Mr. Justice John Sopinka, I contend that pre-Charter rights and freedoms were protected to some degree, but were not as well-protected as they might have been under a written Charter. These same rights now enjoy an enhanced degree of protection via the 1982 Charter.

To gain some sense of the role played by the courts in protected pre-Charter rights and freedoms

We need only turn to the tyrannical era of Quebec Premier Maurice Duplessis. It's here that we find several highly-illustrative examples of accepted Canadian rights being violated by the government of Duplessis only to be restored through the intervention of the courts. As political scientist Ian Greene observes; "the Supreme Court did succeed to some extent protecting civil liberties during the infamous Duplessis era."   1.

Indeed, an example of such success occurred in 1937 after the Quebec legislature enacted its Padlock Law allowing police to lock up any place which was used to distribute information on Communism. John Switzman, a tenant, was locked out of his apartment home for eight years until the Supreme Court ruled that the law was ultra vires as it intruded into federal territory.   2.

Although the above may seem to be a less-than-stirring defence of civil rights, it should be appreciated that in achieving the end of protecting civil rights, judges often prefer to settle cases on the simplest, narrowest grounds available. Thus, if an ultra vires argument protects a right, an ultra vires argument will be used.   3.

We should also appreciate that in the absence of the Canadian Charter of Rights and Freedoms, judges were left without this option and were therefore somewhat manoeuvred into using the means of an ultra vires argument as a quick and effective means of achieving the judicial end of restoration and protection of civil liberties.

Prior to the Charter, Canada was still very much a free and democratic nation which enjoyed the freedoms and rights associated with Great Britain, France, United States and other democratic nations.

Although there were setbacks along the way - including the internment of Canadians of Japanese descent during World War II - Canada's long and established history of respecting freedoms and rights cannot be overlooked.

The Charter, in this regard, adds to an ongoing evolution towards expanded and better-defined rights and freedoms.

As Ronald Cheffins and Patricia Johnson note: "Canada has long recognized a tradition of individual freedom without the necessity of an entrenched Charter of Rights. First, it must be remembered that the starting point of our legal system is that an individual is free except to the extent restrained by law." 4.

Prior to the Charter, the rights and freedoms of Canadians were protected by a combination of statute laws, common laws, precedents and conventions drawing from British and international judicial rulings as well as from the Canadian experience.

In essence, the above amounted to an unwritten Charter, built upon centuries of jurisprudence and culminating in the articulation of principles of justice that we are familiar with today.   5.

The post World War II years in particular yielded a number of important advancements in the recognition and protection of rights affecting various minorities.

For example, regarding the influence of international jurisprudence on Canada's recognition of the right of all people not to be discriminated against on the basis of race, Alan Cairns observes:

> "A host of international conventions, covenants, resolutions, and treaties provides international legitimacy to the principle of non discrimination on grounds of race.   As early as 1945, in Re Drummond Wren, Mr. Justice McKay of the Ontario High Court relied on the UN Charter, the Atlantic Charter, and other domestic and international evidence to strike down a restrictive land covenant barring the selling of land to 'Jews, or to persons of any objectionable nationality.' "   6.

Indeed, the post World War II years leading up to the Charter formed part of an era in which movement regarding the expansion and protection of rights was generally of a forward motion.

Citing several further examples relating to the vote, Cairns adds:

> "The ethnic and racial restrictions in Canadian franchise laws against Chinese, Japanese, East Indians, and Doukhobors were eliminated after 1945. In 1960, status Indians who had previously been denied the franchise on the grounds of its alleged incompatibility with their perceived wardship status, received the vote."   7.

The Charter can thus be seen as part of an evolutionary process in which rights and freedoms were becoming better defined and better entrenched over time. The Charter itself can be viewed in this context as an add-on to the collection of rights enjoyed by Canadians.

The Charter goes beyond any mere cataloguing of existing rights to provide an expanded, constitutionally-entrenched protection of rights and freedoms both at the individual and collective level. In this manner, the Charter represents a further step forward on the rights and freedoms front. As University of Ottawa history professor Michael Behiels notes:

> "The Canadian Charter of Rights and Freedoms is, in many ways, a bold innovative experiment. The Charter, while constitutionalizing individual

rights for all Canadians, does make a valiant attempt to reconcile and harmonize the concepts of individual rights for all and collective rights for certain specific groups in Canadian society." 8

Behiels further observes that the Charter also "recognizes and reinforces the rights and special legal status of minority groups." For example, section 29 reaffirms the right, recognized in the Constitution Act 1867, to schooling in either Protestant or Catholic denominations.   9.

Citing additional areas in which the Charter has protected rights by constitutionally entrenching them, Behiels notes Charter sections 16 through 24 reaffirm and expand on French and English language rights set out in section 133 of the Constitution Act 1867. He adds that section 25 of the Charter and section 35 of the Constitution Act 1982 both "amply," reaffirm the special status given aboriginal people under section 91 (24) of the Constitution Act 1867.   10.

One of the Charter's truly great strengths in terms of further protecting rights and freedoms is that its open-ended and occasionally vague wording invites the Supreme Court to play an activist role in protecting our rights. This role is further strengthened by the fact that our rights and freedoms as Canadians are constitutionally entrenched, giving them dominance over provincial statutes which might otherwise diminish them.

York University Political Science professor
Kenneth McRoberts notes:

> "In fact, it can be argued that the
> Quebec government's position was
> weakened through the Constitution Act
> , 1982. The Charter of Rights and
> Freedoms limits the Quebec
> government's prerogatives in such
> matters as regulating English-language
> schools and restricting access to
> government services by migrants from
> other provinces."   11.

Canadians should take comfort in the fact that
the Charter limits Quebec in the way McRoberts
describes. It is better to have our freedoms and rights
protected by a court operating under principles of
justice and fair play than to leave such fundamental
matters entirely in the hands of politicians so eager to
curry electoral favor that they would willingly
trample on minority rights and by so doing bring
about the tyranny of the majority that our Charter,
the U.S. Bill of Rights and other like documents, seek
to prevent.

An example of such rights-trampling occurred
in Quebec as recently as 1988 with the provincial
government's Bill 101 which, by requiring French-
only commercial signs, succeeded in violating the
basic human right of freedom of expression, protected
under section 2 (B) of the Charter. Adding insult to
injury, the language being restricted was English, one

of Canada's two Official Languages under section 16 (1) of the Charter.   12.

Quebec's actions - which also violated the United Nation's human rights code - were not left unchallenged by the Supreme Court. McRoberts:

> "In December 1988 the Supreme Court of Canada determined that the Bill 101 provision requiring French-only commercial signs was in conflict with the Charter of Rights and Freedoms (as well as Quebec's own Human Rights Act).   13.

Unfortunately, that was not the end of it. As Christopher Manfredi points out:

> "Three days after the Supreme Court struck down the commercial signs provisions of Bill 101 in the Ford decision (December 15, 1988), Quebec Premier Robert Bourassa announced his intention to enact new language legislation (Bill 178) that would be insulated from judicial review by a notwithstanding clause."   14.

Bill 178 allowed the offensive (apparently) English language to be displayed with French provided this usage was confined to the interior of stores and was not outside where everyone could see it. This, of course, did not address the violation of freedom of expression rights of Canadians wishing to use an Official Language without government constraint.

Faced with court determined to uphold the rights and freedoms of Canadians, Bourassa invoked section 33 - the notwithstanding clause - to override the courts and save the law.   15.

Thus, Quebec was able to uphold its odious Law 178 despite the fact that the courts, the U.N. and any other fair-minded entity regards the law as a blatant violation of human rights.

Section 33, as it is currently worded, is in my view a serious flaw in our constitutional apparatus as it allows legislatures relatively unchecked powers (save a five-year time limit) to overrule the fair judicial process employed by our courts regarding the fundamentally important area of human rights.

This might be more acceptable if we could trust our politicians to do what is just and fair but such trust would be unearned: If we have learned anything from more than a century of Canadian politics it is that politicians are by nature prone to currying electoral favor by catering to public opinion - however unfair - in order to maintain office.

Bourassa was reacting to just such 'public pressure' when he introduced Bill 178 which still sought to appease those Quebecers who would deny equal language rights to their fellow citizens. A 1989 poll showed 69 per cent of Quebec francophones felt the provincial government should have the right to restrict Quebec anglophones' freedom of expression even though a vast majority of anglophones did not approve of their rights being so restricted.   16.

The willingness of a majority of Canadian citizens residing in Quebec to violate the freedom of expression of some of their fellow Canadian citizens in the same province speaks clearly of the tyranny of the majority which potentially exists in any given population.

The willingness of the Quebec government to cater to such discrimination and the further willingness of the federal government to condone Quebec's actions both stem from a desire to capture a large portion of the Quebec vote, lending an air of legitimacy to that which is morally unacceptable.

Quebec is not alone in its mistreatment of minorities: Ontario and Manitoba have less than sterling records on matters of language and education rights. Yet as publisher Conrad Black has observed, Quebec has shown a marked tendency to advance a collectivist agenda at the expense of individual rights, from the Duplessis Padlock Law to Bourassa's much-hated Law 178.   17.

Although section 33 of the Charter can be viewed as a troublesome chink in our armour of rights and freedoms, it has not stripped the Charter of its overall ability to give added protection to the many freedoms and rights of Canadians. Indeed, Law 178 is one of very few instances where section 33 has been used to undermine individual Charter rights in a province.

The Charter is not without its critics: Former Manitoba Premier Sterling Lyon had argued, prior to the Charter's passage, that entrenched rights in the Charter would fail to be any better protected than they were prior to the 1982 Charter.   18.

In fact, many cases involving the Charter have resulted in the improved protection - or even expansion - of rights. for example, in the 1989 Andrews Vrs Law Society of British Columbia case, the Supreme Court overruled section 42 (a) of the Barristers and Solicitors Act requiring lawyers in B.C. to be Canadian citizens. In what amounted to an expansion of rights for non-citizens, the Court found the Act violated Charter section 15 equality rights.   19.

Although non-citizenship had not been specifically stated as an area protected from discrimination, an activist Justice Bertha Wilson found that non-citizens were particularly powerless politically and should not be discriminated against in a way affecting their livelihood.   20.

Further examples of entrenched and protected rights are cited by Peter Russell who notes that feminists succeeded in having the Charter rights guaranteed equally to males and females; that those with a mental and physical disability were accorded specific protection, the rights of the criminally accused were strengthened and the onus of proof was placed on governments to justify their encroachments on Charter rights.   21.

As Paul Pross reminds us, the rights and special status of aboriginal people has also received formalized recognition in The Charter.   22.

To gain an even fuller appreciation of the overall power and effectiveness of the Charter in protecting rights and freedoms, and to get a sense of how such protection was limited prior to the Charter, one need only reflect on the very limited impact of another famous piece of Canadian rights legislation: the 1960 Bill of Rights.

The comparative weakness of the Bill of Rights was owed to its status as a mere statute of Parliament and not an amendment to the Constitution Act. As the Bill was limited to the federal government and not the provinces, its effectiveness was further limited beyond its lack of status as anything approximating a supreme law of the land.

All of the Bill's various limitations, cited above, generated judicial problems of application and confusion over its questionable authority and potential usefulness in adjudicating disputes. As Frederick Lee Morton observes:

> "From the start, the Bill of Rights was swamped by problems of interpreta

tion. These problems stemmed princi-
pally from its legal status as an ordinary statute and the ambiguous wording of its second section. Canadian
judges, including those on the Supreme
Court, could not agree on what function the Bill of Rights assigned to the
courts."   23.

Morton further notes that the Canadian Bill of
Rights sole moment of judicial glory arrived with the
1969 Drybones case in which the Supreme Court
found that the Bill gave them the authority to declare
federal statutes invalid. The Court found that section
94 (B) of the Indian Act violated the Indian Drybones
of the right of equality before the law because treated
him more harshly for public intoxication than a non-
native person would be treated.   24.

However, the Drybones case proved to be the
sole example of the Bill of Rights successfully being
used to protect rights. In 1974, the Supreme Court
ignored the Drybones precedent in the Lavell and
Bedard cases to find that these Indian women had
received equality before the law as section 12 (1)(B)
of the Indian Act was equally applied to all native
women by depriving them all of their Indian status
(and accompanying rights to live on reserves) when-
ever they married a non-native. This was considered a
retrograde ruling as it upheld a form of discrimination
that did not apply to Indian men marrying non-native
women.   25.

Thus, the use of the Bill of Rights in adjudicating
cases was severely curtailed from the beginning with
even its limited use - the Drybones case - failing to
even provide the legacy of a a meaningful and
binding precedent. As Patrick Monahan so succinctly
put it:

> "The judicial legacy under the Bill was
> one of endless logical and legal postur-
> ing, apparently designed to ensure that
> the statute's only application would be
> to laws dealing with the drunkenness of
> Indians off their reserves, in the North
> West Territories."   26.

Remarking on the stark contrast between the
judicial self-restraint associated with the Bill of
Rights and the activist approach taken by the Supreme
Court under the 1982 Charter, Monahan suggests
that "the court seems intent on adopting a fundamentally different attitude towards Charter litigation than
it did to cases arising under the Canadian Bill of
Rights."   27.

Indeed, the degree of activism we're now
seeing from the courts under the Charter has
prompted Rainer Knopff and Frederick Morton to
observe:

> "The most striking comparison ... is between
> Charter cases since 1982 and previous civil
> liberties cases arising under the Canadian Bill
> of Rights. The latter instrument, enacted by

the Diefenbaker government in 1960, was
narrower in scope than the Charter because it
applied only to matters within federal jurisdiction. More important, it was an ordinary
statute, not a constitutional document."   28.

Knopff and Morton note that the Charter's
increased usage is owed to its constitutionally entrenched status. In contrast the Bill of Rights had left
judges reluctant to "use an instrument of less than
full constitutional status to invalidate federal legislation.   29.

Knopff and Morton add:
> "Only once between its enactment and
> the coming into effect of the Charter,
> in the 1970 Drybones case, did the
> Supreme Court use the Bill of Rights
> to invalidate a law."   30.

Describing the success of the Charter and the
leeway the courts have given themselves in interpreting it, Monahan observes:
> "Not only has the Charter granted
> relief in over half the cases decided
> thus far, its judgements have been
> robed in the rhetoric of activist judicial
> review. We have been told that the
> Charter is a 'living tree' that must not
> be contaminated by narrow or technical
> interpretation."   31.

Morton offers a more expansive comparison

between the Canadian Bill of Rights and the Charter when he notes that the Supreme Court upheld the rights-claimant in 35 of 100 Charter cases compared with only five of 34 cases concerning the Bill of Rights from the Bill's introduction in 1960 through to 1982 when the Charter came into effect. 32.

Moreover, the introduction of the Charter has had a profound impact on the Court's willingness and ability to play an effective activist role. As Morton observes:

> "Just as the Court's unreceptive attitude towards the 1960 Bill of Rights had the effect of discouraging litigation, the Court's activist jurisprudence under the Charter has stimulated litigation. Since 1987, Charter decisions have accounted for roughly 25 per cent of the Court's annual caseload. 33.

Another indication of the Court's new activism is the number of statutes that it has declared invalid (in whole or in part); 19 by the end of 1989, compared to just one (in Drybones) under the 1960 Bill of Rights." 34.

Noting that Charter cases have won voting rights for the disabled and expanded due process rights for prisoners, Richard Sigurdson concludes:

> "All of these victories for the under-privileged individuals and groups

enhance, rather than undermine, the (beficial) democratic character of our society." 35.

One of the more eloquent statements on the Charter's effectiveness was delivered recently by Mr. Justice John Sopinka, a judge on the Supreme Court of Canada. Commenting on the Charter's strengthening of freedom of speech, Mr. Justice Sopinka observed:

> "Before the Canadian Charter of Rights and Freedoms came into effect, free speech depended for its protection on the force of public opinion and the pressure that it exerted on the legislature... The Charter entrenched the right to freedom of expression in Section 2 (b) ...This provided a specific procedure to enlist the aid of the courts when reedom of speech was under attack by any government action." 36.

It seems only fitting to have called on Mr. Justice Sopinka as this paper's final 'expert witness' offering testimony to the effectiveness of the Charter in protecting the rights and freedoms of Canadians. After all, as observed throughout this paper, the Court has largely abandoned its pre-Charter stance of conservative self-restraint and judicial interpretivism to embrace a much more activist and non-interpretivist approach made possible by the Charter.

Indeed the Charter's ability to provide constitutionally-entrenched and therefore better-protected
freedoms has effectively bolstered the Court's own
freedom to adjudicate Charter cases in an activist
manner.

Throughout the course of this book, Canada's
long-standing tradition of respecting established rights
and freedoms has been recognized, along with recognition of the limited ability of an essentially unwritten-Charter to fully protect these treasured aspects of
Canadian life.

We have also explored the federal government's
attempt to address this issue with the introduction of
the Canadian Bill of Rights in 1960 which provided a
more formalized cataloguing of existing rights and
freedoms.

Yet we've also seen that the Bill's status as a
mere statute left it unable to fully protect rights and
freedoms to the same extent that a constitutionally-
entrenched document such as the 1982 Charter is
effectively able to achieve.

As well, we've explored the Court's reluctance
to rely on the Bill of Rights, rarely choosing to use
this document, in marked contrast to the considerably
more frequent usage given the Charter.

Finally, this book has shown that the constitutionally-entrenched 1982 Charter has been used to

successfully protect and uphold, and in some cases expand, the rights and freedoms of Canadians. We've also seen how this protective power of the Charter has been effectively used by the Court to effectively save rights and freedoms through non-interpretivism and judicial activism.

We can therefore conclude that although Canada enjoyed a long history of rights and freedoms before the Charter, and although these same rights and freedoms were accorded the protection of years of jurisprudence, precedents and a virtual unwritten-Charter, and although these rights were further enhanced by the Bill of Rights, the rights and freedoms of Canadians still received better protection after the 1982 Charter.

Rights and freedoms therefore existed and were protected before the Charter - but they were not as well-protected.

The 1982 Charter marks a momentous step forward in Canada's evolution towards more formalized freedoms and rights.

With its formal setting out of rights and its inherent, constitutionally-entrenched power, the Charter, through the Court, is effectively ensuring the rights and freedoms of Canadians are better defined - and better protected.

End Notes:

For Chapter Three

1. Ian Greene, The Charter of Rights, Toronto: James Lorimer & Company, Publishers, 1989, p. 21.

2. IBID, p. 22.

3. IBID, p. 5.

4. R. I. Cheffins & P. A. Johnson, The Revised Canadian Constitution. Politics As Law, Toronto: McGraw-Hill Ryerson Limited, 1986, p. 132.

5. IBID, pp. 1-69.

6. Alan C. Cairns, Charter Versus Federalism. The Dilemmas of Constitutional Reform, Montreal: McGill-Queen's University Press, 1992, p. 25.

7. Alan C. Cairns, Charter Versus Federalism. The Dilemmas of Constitutional Reform, ontreal: McGill-Queen's University Press, 1992, p. 25.

8. Michael D. Behiels, 'From the Constitution Act, 1982 to the Meech Lake Accord, 1987: Individual Rights for All versus Collective Rights for Some' from 'Democracy With Justice, edited by Alain-G. Gagnon and A. Brian Tanguay, Ottawa: Carleton University Press, 1992, p. 127.

9. IBID, p. 128.

10. Michael D. Behiels, 'From the Constitution Act, 1982 to the Meech Lake Accord, 1987: Individual Rights for All versus Collective Rights for Some' from 'Democracy With Justice, edited by Alain-G. Gagnon and A. Brian Tanguay, Ottawa: Carleton University Press, 1992, p. 128.

11. Kenneth McRoberts, Quebec: Province, Nation, or 'Distinct Society'?' from Canadian Politics in the 1990s, Third Edition edited by Michael S. Whittington and Glen Williams. Toronto: Nelson Canada, 1990. p. 115.

12. Canadian Charter of Rights and Freedoms, 1982, sections 2 (B) and 16 (1) cited.

13. Kenneth McRoberts, Quebec: Province, Nation, or 'Distinct Society'?' from Canadian Politics in the 1990s, Third Edition edited by Michael S. Whittington and Glen Williams. Toronto: Nelson Canada, 1990. p. 115.

14. Christopher P. Manfredi, Judicial Power And The Charter, Toronto: McClelland & Stewart Inc., 1993. p. 202.

15. Kenneth McRoberts, Quebec: Province, Nation, or 'Distinct Society'?' from Canadian Politics in the 1990s, Third Edition edited by Michael S. Whittington and Glen Williams. Toronto: Nelson Canada, 1990. p. 115.

16. 'Language Law Poll Finds Most Opposed', The Toronto Star, January 22, 1989. p. A19.

17. Conrad Black, 'Canada: A Fragile Nation', from Canadian Politics 91/92, edited by Gregory S. Mahler & Roman March, Guilford: Dushkin Publishing, 1991, pp. 8-9.

18. David Milne, The Canadian Constitution, Toronto: James Lorimer & Company, 1991. pp. 89-91.

19. Peter H. Russell, Rainer Knopff and Ted Morton, Federalism and the Charter, Ottawa: Carleton University Press, 1993. pp. 582-590.

20. Peter H. Russell, Rainer Knopff and Ted Morton, Federalism and the Charter, Ottawa: Carleton University Press, 1993. pp. 582-590.

21. Peter H. Russell, Constitutional Odyssey, Can Canadians Become a Sovereign People? Toronto: Univesity of Toronto Press, 1992. p. 114.

22. A. Paul Pross, Group Politics and Public Policy, Second Edition, Toronto: Oxford University Press, 1992. p. 181.

23. F. L. Morton, Law, Politics and the Judicial Process in Canada, Second Edition, edited by F. L. Morton, Calgary: University of Calgary Press, 1992. p. 398.

24. IBID. p. 399.

25. IBID.

26. Patrick Monahan, Politics and Constitutional Interpretation', from Crosscurrents, Contem porary Political Issues, edited by Mark Charlton and Paul Barker, Scarborough: Nelson Canada, 1991. p. 86.

27. IBID.

28. Rainer Knopff and F. L. Morton, Charter Politics, Scarborough: Nelson Canada, 1992. p. 19.

29. IBID.
30. IBID.

31. Patrick Monahan, Politics and Constitutional Interpretation', from Crosscurrents, Contem porary Political Issues, edited by Mark Charlton and Paul Barker, Scarborough: Nelson Canada, 1991. p. 86.

32. F. L. Morton, Law, Politics and the Judicial Process in Canada, Second Edition, edited by F. L. Morton, Calgary: University of Calgary Press, 1992. p. 401.

33. IBID.
34. IBID.

35. Richard Sigurdson, 'Left -and-Ring-Wing Charterphobia in Canada: A Critique of the Critics' from a paper delivered at the Canadian Political Science Association annual meeting, Charlottetowne, PEI, May 31, 1992. p. 23.

36. John Sopinka, 'Free Speech; Its limits and its opponents', from The Hamilton Spectator, Tuesday, November 2, 1993. p. A11.

CHAPTER FOUR

The collapse of David Peterson's Government:

Was Peterson's support for decentralizing accords a factor in his defeat?

Consciously or unconsciously, many Canadians favour a strong central government at the federal level.

This is seldom directly indicated in public opinion polls since the question of centralization is rarely – if ever – bluntly raised. It's doubtful many Canadians would necessarily know how to respond even if the question was raised in such a fashion.

Instead, support for a strong central government appears indirectly, through public opposition to federal-provincial initiatives such as the decentralizing Charlottowne and Meech Lake accords. Public opinion was strongly against these pacts.

Although few Canadians would have cited the accords' decentralizing nature for their opposition, many did cite a reluctance to see more federal powers given to Quebec and the other provinces – and this amounts to decentralization.

Despite a willingness on the part of many Canadians to accommodate Quebec, many people feel most comfortable with a strong central government.

They want the federal government to be capable of representing the interests of the nation as a whole, both at home and abroad. They resent the idea that provinces might independently compete with Canada on the world stage.

Consider, for example, the public backlash to Quebec initiatives to have athletes from that province compete against other Canadians at the Olympic Games (the backlash was strong enough to kill that initiative), or public anger over Quebec insisting on wooing and screening immigrants to that province (something which has taken place and that politicians are downplaying to avoid a stiff backlash).

Perhaps one of the more compelling arguments to be made about public support for centralization and – by extension – opposition to decentralization, can be

found in the dramatic election loss suffered by David Peterson's Ontario Liberals. Peterson had supported the decentralizing accords and paid a heavy political price for doing so.

To examine Peterson's electoral defeat, I'm including a 1993 book review written for Professor Andre Turcotte concerning the book Not Without Cause. Although there were other factors leading to the Peterson government's collapse, the premier's support of decentralizing accords was certainly a major contributor to his defeat. The book review follows:

Not Without Flaws...A Book Review of Not Without Cause
Review by Michael B. Davie

Georgette Gagnon & Dan Rath, Not Without Cause; David Peterson's Fall From Grace, Toronto: Harper and Collins Publishers Ltd., 1991.

The sudden, staggering defeat of David Peterson's Liberal government in 1990 at the hands of the Ontario electorate caught many by surprise and left political observers searching for answers.

Why had a majority government led by a personable, once-popular leader been brought down so dramatically? So complete was this historic, political annihilation, that the Liberal government was swept away in an NDP landslide which even captured Peterson's own London Centre riding. Faced with these dramatic results and without a seat of his own in the legislature, Peterson promptly resigned from his party's leadership and left political life.

Was public dissatisfaction over a clearly-opportunist election call still early in his mandate the main reason for Peterson's fall?

Or was it the government's policies, perceived inertia, Meech Lake Accord retribution, or some combination of these factors which brought the Peterson Liberal government down?

In an attempt to answer these questions, Rath, a print and television journalist formerly with TV11 in Hamilton, and Gagnon, the former chief of staff to the Solicitor General, have delved behind the scenes and interviewed backroom campaign strategists, pollsters and key politicians.

As a result of these efforts, the authors have created an informative, descriptive account of the events and circumstances behind the fall of Peterson's Liberal government in Ontario. Not Without Cause remains the most comprehensive treatment of the Peterson government collapse.

Not Without Cause offers an intimate portrait of a fallen Ontario Liberal leader who
achieved much during a two-year accord with the
NDP but accomplished little in the majority Liberal
government which followed.

Although I will later take issue with some of
the finer points in Not Without Cause, it must be
stated here that the broad brushstrokes in this candid
portrait have swept the political canvas with flair and
accuracy: Peterson is depicted as shamelessly op-
portunistic when offering only vague generalities to
defend his fateful decision to call an election just
three years into a majority mandate which had yielded
little of substance.

There is much validity in the book's underlying premise that this unnecessary election call
prompted an electoral backlash of protest voting
which had the clearly unforeseen result of producing
a majority NDP government.

As well, the authors succeed in boldly outlin-
ing other factors such as the Patty Starr fund-raising
scandal, confrontations with angry interest groups, an
ailing economy and fed-up voters, all of which certainly contributed heavily to the Liberal government's
demise.

The effective presentation of these issues
throughout the book amounts to an informal examination of Peterson's political fortunes within the

Public Choice approach. In this regard, it is possible to see Peterson as a victim of high public expectations confronting diminishing resources and an inability of governments at all levels to maintain, let alone enhance, services.

Not Without Cause offers a largely-journalistic account which also provides some limited analysis based on an abundance of opinion polls undertaken during the course of the Peterson government's tenure.

In this regard it attempts more than a retelling of what went wrong as it tries to explain why events unfolded as they did. Not Without Cause is also well-presented and well-written. Its many strengths make it essential reading for anyone interested in Ontario politics and I would recommend this book to anyone desiring some intriguing insight into the perplexing collapse of a once-popular government. The compilation of expert opinions throughout this book add up to a thought-provoking retrospective of a fateful period in Ontario politics.

Yet as the title of this review suggests, some caution is advised as the authors' work is not without flaws: Although the views of insiders and participants are utilized to strong advantage, it's worth noting that these same insiders readily admit that they were woefully out of touch with the true inclinations of the electorate and made a number of serious misjudgements.

Indeed, their very closeness to the Peterson campaign may have left them unable to see the forest of voter dissent for the trees of more immediate concerns such as election debates and campaign speeches. It is a mistake therefore to rely to such a strong extent on their viewpoints.

Although a few non-Liberal campaign sources are cited in this book, including leaders of the other political parties, the authors have relied heavily on the views of insiders to the near-exclusion of outside experts, not tied so closely to the campaign, who might have been able to offer a more detached and balanced assessment.

The authors have also chosen to give considerable (and in their book, unchallenged) weight to their own opinions as to what went wrong with the Peterson campaign and these views are again based mainly on interviews with insiders.

Simply put, the authors missed the opportunity to seek the analysis of outside experts and political scientists whose interpretations might have provided further insight into the 1990 election and given this work added depth.

As well, Not Without Cause could have provided a fuller analysis of the Meech Lake factor beyond its repeated observations that not everyone was happy with Peterson's role in the ill-fated accord and that it obsessed the premier to an unhealthy degree. The authors even repeat Peterson's shallow observation that the voters were "cranky."

In fact, it does the voters of Ontario a great disservice and is an insult to their collective intelligence to suggest that anger directed at the premier over the Meech Lake Accord was due to some sort of ill-defined "crankiness" or unhappiness with the amount of time the premier spent on the ill-fated accord.

The Meech Lake issue must be viewed in its wider context: Accord negotiations followed Quebec's controversial Bill 101 language law which, among other things, restricted the use of the English language on signs and was a violation of the basic human right of freedom of expression, as the United Nations would later assert.

Bills 101 and 178 rendering the official language spoken by the vast majority of Canadians less acceptable in one corner of Canada, did not sit at all well with Canadians who view their country as a country, and not a loose collection of provinces.

As Rand Dyck observes in Provincial Politics in Canada, the Supreme Court of Canada subsequently found the sign law unconstitutional and a violation of Quebec's own Charter of Rights (Rand Dyck, 1991: p. 265).

Whatever comfort this ruling might have provided to anyone's sense of fair play proved short-lived: Quebec Premier Robert Bourassa promptly invoked the Canadian Constitution's notwithstanding clause to overrule the highest court in the land and enact a language law that was unacceptable to many Canadians.

For many Canadians, including some otherwise sympathetic and supportive of Quebec efforts to preserve and protect the French language, the sign law triggered a sense of betrayal, heightened distrust of Quebec and raised profound fears of separation. This of course had an immediate impact on the Meech Lake Accord talks. As Dyck notes: "many non-Quebeckers who had been ambivalent about the Accord began to oppose it." (Rand Dyck, 1991: p. 265).

Importantly, the Meech Lake circumstances I've just outlined are absent from Not Without Cause. Also absent is any reference to Peterson's press conference with Bourassa in which he promised the Quebec premier that whatever happened regarding Quebec separation, Ontario could be counted on to continue close economic ties.

Many Canadians viewed this hasty pledge as an unseemly near-endorsement of separation at a time when politicians were being called on to cease condoning and start questioning both Quebec's actions and the apparent effort to accommodate Quebec regardless of the decentralizing cost to Canada.

In The Provincial State, Keith Brownsey and Michael Howlett note that "Peterson found himself defending an agreement that was criticized as undemocratic and decentralizing," while the closed-door negotiating process was viewed with suspicion in an open political system (Keith Brownsey and Michael Howlett, 1992: p. 165).

Although Gagnon and Rath also noted that the secretive process was criticized, their failure to otherwise explore the circumstances surrounding Meech Lake opposition has exposed the shallowness of their understanding of the Accord's impact on Peterson's downfall. The Accord was undoubtedly an important factor behind the Liberal collapse yet it receives only superficial treatment in Not Without Cause.

Another shortcoming in this generally-insightful book is its lack of historical analysis which might have placed the events related to Peterson's fall in perspective.

The timeframe employed is tightly confined to the period following the collapse of Frank Miller's Progressive Conservative government in 1985, through to the subsequent two-year-long Liberal-NDP accord government of Liberals, on to the Liberal Majority government of 1987 and ending with the Liberals' crushing defeat in 1990.

The problem with this limited timeframe is that the brief references made to the Tory Ontario of Peterson's youth make the subsequent, dramatic changes from 1985 to 1990 seem far more remarkable than they actually are.

As Brownsey and Howlett note, the shift away from the Tories to favor the Liberals and NDP in Key ridings such in Toronto, Hamilton and London had been steadily building since the 1960s as Ontario became more multi-cultural and less enamoured with a PC party viewed as favoring an Anglo Saxon business elite. The NDP share of the popular vote and seats has also been increasing, to the extent that this third party became the Official Opposition in 1975. (Brownsey & Howlett, 1992: pp. 156-163).).

At first glance the 38 years of Tory dominance that preceded Peterson give Ontario the image of a complacent, self-satisfied province which was only too happy to routinely return the ruling Conservatives election after election, perpetuating a remarkable political dynasty.

However, a closer examination of Ontario politics shows that during this entire timespan from 1943 to 1985, the Tories have never won a majority of the popularity vote, meaning more Ontarions have voted against the party than for it during the full length of its 38-year tenure.

Of 13 elections during this period, only three

succeeded in capturing 48-49 per cent of the popular vote while the rest produced results of 45 per cent or less. Four of the resulting governments - about a third of the 13 PC governments - were minority governments with only 36-37 per cent of the popular vote (Rand Dyck, 1991: pp. 341-349).

The Tories had also become experts at accommodating the electorate's desire for change over the years by skilfully changing leaders in a process of regeneration.

As recent history has shown, a flaw in the short-lived Miller government was that that change of leadership from Bill Davis to Frank Miller had failed to successfully convey an image of renewal. Instead, voters saw the old premier being replaced by an even older man whose small-town Tory views were considered out-of-step with the times (Rand Dyck, 1991: pp. 317-330).

From all of this, we can surmise that the voters of Ontario have been less complacent than electoral outcomes would suggest. This in turn reveals the importance of changing demographics emphasizing non-Charter group minorities and swing voters who can make or break governments in the three-way races that have characterized Ontario politics.

Yet, the underlying political trends and Tory strategies I've just outlined are missing from Not Without Cause and this omission opens the risk of leaving gaps in the reader's understanding of how and why Ontario's political culture could have produced a Peterson landslide followed by a Peterson collapse just three years later.

This lack of historical analysis lends, by default, a disproportionate amount of weight to the authors' underlying premise that the rise and fall of Peterson was in large part hinged on the Liberal leader's personal popularity.

Indeed, the book's title is taken from a line in William Shakespeare's Julius Caesar: "You all did love him once, not without cause." In the interest of clarity, Not Without Cause should have provided a more clearly defined historical context in which to judge the events leading up to and beyond the collapse of Peterson's majority government.

Having pointed out the chief flaws in Not Without Cause, let me assert once again that I would still highly recommend this book for anyone interested in gaining a fuller understanding of the collapse of the Peterson Liberal government in Ontario.

Despite the various limitations cited throughout this review, Not Without Cause remains the only book to provide such a detailed and comprehensive look at Peterson's fall from grace.

If read in conjunction with the articles cited in this review, the book's limitations can easily be addressed, leaving the reader free to appreciate its many strengths. With its lean writing style, reliance on colorful quotations and dramatic pacing, Not Without Cause succeeds in painting the events of 1990 in memorable, human terms.

This book still shines as a skilful, moment-by-moment chronicle of a government's rapid slide into arrogance and inertia framed within the political issues and scandals of the day - and with numerous glimpses into the backroom machinations of an unsteady political machine.

The book's ability to probe the infighting of campaign organizers and scrutinize Peterson's vacillating and excessively consultative leadership style are real strengths that make Not Without Cause well worth reading.

As well, the authors have shed new light on the NDP's smear campaign against Peterson which served to undermine his credibility and popularity.

Combined with effective attacks from an otherwise shattered and meagre Tory party, the negative attention focused on Peterson would prove devastating at a time when many Canadians were fed up with government at all levels.

Not Without Cause also effectively illustrates the image transformation of Peterson from a somewhat nerdish-looking, overweight, inadequate public speaker into a slim, polished television communicator exuding confidence. The book then unveils, with stunning clarity, the degree to which political images can also be broken.

Although I have taken issue with the book's limited scope and found fault with its narrowness of interpretation and analysis, the strengths of Not Without Cause largely compensate for its analytical weaknesses.

After all is said, the book succeeds in providing a wealth of truly insightful, behind-the-scenes observations in a clearly-stated manner which is at once informative and engaging to the reader.

For intriguing insight into the collapse of a provincial government, Not Without Cause is, without question, a compelling place to begin. It serves as profound warning to politicians everywhere to temper their faith in opinion polls and never take the voters for granted.

"Unable to effectively represent Canadian interests, our federal government is at risk of having its strings pulled by foreign powers – assuming, of course, that the provinces loosen their own grip long enough for that to happen."

- **Michael B. Davie**

CONCLUSION

Paying the high cost of decentralization:
The Canadian nation may be reduced to a hollow shell

By this point, I hope that you now share this writer's concerns about the excessive decentralization of Canada.

Still not convinced?
Perhaps you should revisit the puppet governments of Europe during times of war.

Hitler enjoyed installing such puppet government in the countries he conquered.

Although these governments often gave the appearance of being legitimate and effective, Hitler controlled the strings, making the leaders dance to his tune. These fake governments created a false sense of continuity and security in their domestic populations, lulling them in believing all was well. The puppet government lent a veneer of credibility to atrocities. I concealed the true extent of the Nazi menace.

The puppet government often gave the outward apperance of being a functioning national government – but all the important decisions were made in Germany.

I'm not suggesting Canada has been reduced to a puppet government – but the threat is certainly real. Beyond the powers Canada has surrendered to the provinces, our nation has also surrended much of its fomer sovereignty to international trade agreements with the United States. We might be able to afford such a loss if our country was otherwise strong. But it is weak and decentralized.

Unable to effectively represent Canadian interests, our federal government is at risk of having its strings pulled by foreign powers – assuming, of course, that the provinces loosen their own grip long enough for that to happen.

Canada began with its federal government functioning as a central, national government. It was clearly the superior, senior level of government and the

provinces were subordinate to the federal government.
Our federal government was so clearly superior, it even had the right to strike down provincial laws that were not to its liking.

Yet all of this was undermined through a series of court ruling and by federal governments eager to gain favour with the provinces. Over time, many federal powers were stripped and the provinces became ever more powerful.

Even when the federal government attempted to appease Quebec alone by granting that single province additional powers, this was invariably met with a concerted demand from the other provinces for equal treatment. The result: All of the provinces gained powers they never should have had – at maximum cost to the federal government.

We've even witnessed the sorry display of Quebec politicians demanding that Quebec athletes compete against Canadian athletes at the Olympic Games.

Although this hasn't come to pass – as yet – it does provide an indication of how far province-building can really go.

Already, Quebec has its own immigration offices operating side-by-side with federal offices, giving potential immigrants the choice of emmigrating to Canada – or Quebec!

How much longer can we allow this to continue at the expense of our national government?

We can hope the tide of decentralization will soon come to an end. We can also tell our politicians we want a strong central government. This message needs to be heard not only by federal members, but also by provincial members.

Our politicians at every level need a reminder from all of us that we are first and foremost Canadians who need and demand a strong central government that is committed to representing all of Canada.

- Michael B. Davie.

BIBLIOGRAPHY

Beck, J. M., The Shaping of Canadian Federalism: Central Authority or Provincial Right? Toronto: The Copp Clark Publishing Company, 1971.

Behiels, Michael D., 'From the Constitution Act, 1982 to the Meech Lake Accord, 1987: Individual Rights for All versus Collective Rights for Some' from Democracy With Justice, edited by Alain-G. Gagnon and A. Brian Tanguay, Ottawa: Carleton University Press, 1992.

Black, Conrad, 'Canada: A Fragile Nation', from Canadian Politics 91/92, edited by Gregory S. Mahler & Roman March, Guilford: Dushkin, 1991.

Black, Edwin R., 'Supreme Court Judges as Spear-Carriers for Ottawa: They need Watching,' from Report on Confederation, February, 1978.

Brodie, Janine, 'Tensions from Within: Regionalism and Party Politics in Canada', from Party Politics in Canada 6th Ed., edited by Hugh G. Thorburn, Toronto: Prentice-Hall Canada, 1991.

Brown Craig, 'The Nationalism of the National Policy,' from Readings in Canadian History. Post-Confederation, edited by R. Douglas Francis & Donald B. Smith, Toronto: Holt, Rinehart and Winston of Canada, 1990.

Cairns, Alan C., 'The Judicial Committee and Its Critics,' from Federalism in Canada. Selected Readings, edited by Garth Stevenson, Toronto: McClelland & Stewart Inc., 1989.

Cairns, Alan C., Charter Versus Federalism. The Dilemmas of Constitutional Reform, Montreal: McGill-Queen's University Press, 1992.

Cameron, Duncan, and Smith, Miriam, Constitutional Politics, Toronto: Canada, 1992.

Canadian Charter of Rights and Freedoms, 1982.

Cheffins, R. I. & P.A. Johnson, The Revised Canadian Constitution, Toronto: McGraw-Hill Ryerson Ltd., 1986.

Cholewinski, Richard., Human Rights In Canada: Into the 1990s and Beyond, Ottawa: Human Rights Research and Education Centre, 1990.

Clarke, Harold, D., Jane Jenson, Lawrence Le Duc & Jon H. Pammett, Absent Mandate, Toronto: Gage Educational Publishing Company, 1991.

Francis, R. Douglas, Richard Jones & Donald B. Smith, Origins. Canadian History To Confederation, Toronto: Holt, Rinehart & Winston Canada Ltd., 1988.

Francis, R. Douglas, Richard Jones & Donald B. Smith, Destinies. Canadian History Since Confederation, Toronto: Holt, Rinehart and Winston of Canada Ltd., 1988.

Georgette Gagnon & Dan Rath, Not Without Cause; David Peterson's Fall From Grace, Toronto: Harper and Collins Publishers, 1991.

Gibbons, Roger, Conflict & Unity, Toronto: Nelson, 1990.

Greene, Ian, The Charter of Rights, Toronto: James Lorimer & Company, Publishers, 1989.

Greenwood, F., Murray, 'Lord Watson, Institutional Self-Interest and the Decentralization of Canadian Federalism in the 1890s', in University of British Columbia Law Review, 9, 1974.

Kennedy, W. P. M., Essays in Constitutional Law, London: Oxford University Press, 1934.

Knopff, Rainer, and Morton, F. L., Charter Politics, Scarborough: Nelso: 1990.

LaSelva, Samuel V., 'Only in Canada: Federalism, Non Obstante and the Charer from Perspectives on Canadian Federalism, Toronto: James Lorimer & Company, 1992

Laskin, Bora, 'Peace, Order and Good Government re-examined', in Canadian Bar Review, 25, 1947.

Manfredi, Christopher P., Judicial Power And The Charter, Toronto: Mclelland and Stewart, 1993.

McNaught, Kenneth , The Penguin History of Canada, (Markham: Penguin Books Canada Ltd., 1988.

McRoberts, Kenneth, Quebec: Province, Nation, or 'Distinct Society'?' from Canadian Politics in the 1990s, 3rd Ed. edited by Michael Whittington & Glen Williams. Toronto: Nelson Canada, 1990.

Meekison, Peter, 'The Amending Formula,' from Perspectives on Canadian Federalism, edited R. D. Olling & M. W. Westmacott, Toronto: Prentice Hall, 1988.

Milne, David, The Canadian Constitution, Toronto: James Lorimer & Co., 1991.

Monahan, Patrick, Politics and Constitutional Interpretation', from Crosscurrents, Contemporary Political Issues, edited by Mark Charlton and Paul Barker, Scarborough: Nelson Canada, 1991.

Morton, F. L., Law, Politics and the Judicial Process in Canada, Second Edition, Calgary: University of Calgary Press, 1992.

Politics As Law, Toronto: McGraw-Hill Ryerson Limited, 1986.

Pross, Paul A., Group Politics and Public Policy, 2nd Ed., Toronto: Oxford University Press, 1992.

Readings in Canadian History. Pre-Confederation, Toronto: Holt, Rinehart and Winston of Canada, 1990.

Reuber, Grant ,L., 'Federalism and Negative-Sum Games' from Confederation In Crisis, edited by Robert Young, Toronto: James Lorimer, 1991.

Russell, Peter H., Constitutional Odyssey, Can Canadians Become a Sovereign People? Toronto: University of Toronto Press, 1992.

Russell, Peter H.; Knopff, Rainer; and Morton, Ted, Federalism and the Charter, Ottawa: Carleton University Press, 1993.

Scott, F. R., 'Centralization and Decentralization in Canadian Federalism,' from Federalism in Canada, edited by Garth Stevenson, Toronto: McClelland & Stewart Inc., 1989.

Scott, F. R., 'Political Nationalism and Confederation,' Canadian Journal of Economics and Political Science, VIII, August, 1942.

Scott, Frank, R., 'The Privy Council and Mr. Bennett's 'New Deal' Legislation', in F. R. Scott, Essays on the Constitution, Toronto: University of Toronto Press, 1977.

Sigurdson, Richard, 'Left -and-Ring-Wing Charterphobia in Canada: A Critique of the Critics' from a paper delivered at the Canadian Political Science Association meeting, Charlottetowne, PEI, May 31, 1992.

Simeon, Richard, 'Considerations on Centralization and Decentralization', from Perspectives on Canadian Federalism, edited by R. D. Olling and M. W. Westmacott, Scarborough: Prentice-Hall Canada Inc., 1988.

Simeon, Richard and Ian Robinson, State, Society, and the Development of Canadian Federalism, Toronto: University of Toronto Press, 1990.

Simeon, Richard, 'Concluding Comments,' from Canadian Federalism: Meeting Global Economic Challenges?' edited by Douglas M. Brown and M. G. Smith, Kingston: Queen's University, 1991.

Smiley, Donald, V. , The Federal Condition In Canada, Toronto: McGrawHill Ryerson, 1987.

Sopinka, John, 'Free Speech; Its limits and its opponents', from The Hamilton Spectator, Tuesday, November 2, 1993.

Stevenson, Garth, Unfulfilled Union: Canadian Federalism and National Unity, Toronto: Gage Educational Publishing Company, 1989.

Stevenson, Garth, 'Federalism and Intergovernmental Relations,' from Canadian Politics in the 1990s, 3rd Ed., Toronto: Nelson Canada, 1990.

Stevenson, Garth, Unfulfilled Union: Canadian Federalism and National Unity, (Toronto: Gage Educational Publishing Company, 1989), p. 29.

Taylor, Charles, 'Shared and Divergent Values', from Options for a New Canada, edited by Ronald L. Watts and Douglas M. Brown, Toronto: University of Toronto Press, 1991.

The Toronto Star, January 22, 1989.

Trudeau, Pierre, Elliott, Federalism And The French Canadians, Toronto: The Macmillan Company of Canada Ltd., 1968.

Watts, Ronald, L., and Brown, Douglas, M., Options for a New Canada, Toronto: University of Toronto Press, 1991.

Webster's New World Dictionary, David B. Guralnik, Editor in Chief, (New York: Simon and Schuster Inc., 1984), p. 231.

Wheare, K. C., Federal Government, London: Oxford University Press, 1946.

Whitaker, Reg, 'The Overriding Right,' from Canadian Politics 91/92, edited by Gregory S. Mahler and Roman R. March, Guilford, Conn.: Dushkin Publishing Group, 1991.

www.ingramcontent.com/pod-product-compliance
Lightning Source LLC
Chambersburg PA
CBHW021834020426
42334CB00014B/617